RESCUE!

RESCUE!

TRUE STORIES FROM LAKE DISTRICT MOUNTAIN RESCUE

_____

JOHN WHITE

Constable · London

First published in Great Britain 1997
by Constable and Company Limited
3 The Lanchesters, 162 Fulham Palace Road
London W6 9ER
Copyright © John White
ISBN 0 09 476720 3
The right of John White to be identified as author
of this work has been asserted by him in accordance with
the Copyright, Designs and Patents Act 1988
Set in Linotron Palatino $10\frac{1}{2}$ pt by
CentraCet, Saffron Walden
Printed in Great Britain by
St Edmundsbury Press Ltd
Bury St Edmunds, Suffolk

A CIP catalogue record for this book
is available from the British Library

This book is dedicated to the real heroes in Mountain Rescue,
the unheard of majority who turn out whatever the weather
and whatever the time of day, to help their fellow mountaineers;
and to my three lads, Jack, Rob and Luke

ACKNOWLEDGEMENTS

Thanks are due to Bill Birkett for helping give me the confidence to write this and to the Langdale Ambleside Mountain Rescue Team for giving me the experience to draw on. In particular I would like to thank my wife, Gill, for her patience and encouragement.

CONTENTS

LIST OF ILLUSTRATIONS

1

A TALE OF
TWO CALL-OUTS

We were anticipating a sumptuous feast that night at the Old Dungeon Ghyll Hotel in Langdale, where the Abraham Club, a loosely knit band of local climbers, were holding their incomparable annual dinner. Named after George and Ashley, the famous Abraham brothers of Keswick and important pioneers of both early rock climbing and photography, the club never held official meets, had no committee or hierarchy, possessed nothing and had no members. Indeed, to claim to have been a member of the Abraham Club would have been the most effective method of saying that you did not belong to it! Despite this, we attracted guest speakers as famous as Chris Bonington and as humorous as Tony Greenbank and Paul Ross – both legends in the rock climbing world. Many associated with the club were brilliant climbers, and at the very least the majority shared the same enthusiasm and burning energy for climbing.

In order to give our appetites the necessary resolve for one of Neil Walmsley's renowned 'pork-outs', I decided to venture into the damp afternoon to climb a few routes on Raven Crag with Bill Birkett, a strong local climber from Little Langdale, whose father Jim climbed the first Extreme rock climb in the area. Directly above the hotel and a couple of hundred feet high and with dozens of excellent climbs, Raven is well-suited to those cragrats for whom the evening's beer is as important as the aesthetics of being on a lonely mountain cliff – not that we would fall into this category of course!

The routes passed smoothly by – Bilberry Buttress, Evening Wall, Original Route – and though we climbed competently and with great speed, there was a slight dampness about the rock which tightened the concentration, and I recall feeling slightly uneasy on the Original Route at the end of a 150-foot run out of rope, a feeling noted but discarded as the total commitment and concentration necessary for safe and successful climbing took over. A couple of hours and several hundred feet of climbing later, we descended for the final time to the foot of the crag, removed our toe-crushing rock boots with the usual accompaniment of relief, and quickly packed the gear away before trundling down the blocky scree slope towards the hotel and some much-needed refreshment.

There exists a version of the well-known sod's law in relation to rescues. The more desperate you are to eat/drink/sleep/go out/ have a quiet night in, the more likely the bleeper is to emit its shrill twitter, so similar incidentally to that which marks the end of each *Mastermind* contestant's turn in the hot seat that many team members have unwittingly rushed for their boots and rucsacs as Magnus Magnusson recited his well-practised 'I've started so I'll finish.' This is all very well if you are at home on your own, but deeply embarrassing if you have visitors, who then proceed to find other ways of imitating the sound of the bleeper in order to have a good laugh at your subsequent reactions.

The bleeper on this occasion sounded well before we had the opportunity to pass through the oak doors of the Old Dungeon, and in answer to its demand I dragged an unwilling Bill to the foot of Stickle Ghyll where the team were meeting. The usual early arrivals who either lived close by and drove like demonically possessed rally drivers, or who, having nothing better to do, hung around the rescue base just in case there should be a call-out, had already set off up the ghyllside path with a selection of climbing gear, no doubt hoping that someone who could use it would be close behind! The report we were given was that someone had become cragfast on Pavey Ark, a 600-foot buttress of volcanic rock overlooking Stickle Tarn. The mightiest crag in Langdale and one of the finest in the region, Pavey Ark, is criss-crossed with climbs of all standards and, though it offers a well-known easy scramble called Jack's Rake across its front, anyone straying from this without climbing experience would be likely to get into some serious and unforgiving terrain. With little information on the exact location of the casualty and with darkness not too far away, Bill and I huffed and puffed to the foot of the crag in half an hour, and from here we could see the stranded person – a tiny figure about whom we knew very little at this stage, except that his position was precarious to say the least, perched on a heathery ledge 150 feet above Jack's Rake and 350 above the ground.

Scrambling nimbly up the Rake, we soon came upon a group of rescuers huddled at a widening below a climb called Cook's Tour which seemed to offer the only practicable way of reaching him from below. Another group had already departed for the top of Pavey Ark, from where they hoped to descend by abseil. This was a sound tactic, though the scale of the crag meant that such an access would be difficult and that the exact position of the stranded person could be awkward to gauge. Fortunately, the party included Colyn Earnshaw, one of the most experienced rescuers in the country and a very capable climber.

I made the judgement that it would be quicker and easier to reach the casualty from below, though some would say that this was a ploy to avoid walking up to the crag top – climbers are notoriously lazy! There were problems associated with this mode of attack. I had no climbing boots, just studded training shoes which would have all the attributes of roller skates on the greasy rock I would encounter, and the route itself passed a few yards to one side of the casualty with a completely unknown section of rock between the two.

A quick piece of bartering with Jim Fuller, our local electrical goods retailer and as sober and reliable an individual as could be found in the team, brought me some decent footwear, and though it was not a deal he approved of – rather like exchanging his latest hi-tech colour TV for an old black and white set – his masonic concern for getting to the casualty speedily overrode his natural reluctance. Now attired in good walking boots, a harness, helmet and adorned with a vast array of technical gear, I was able to start climbing towards the lonely figure.

Bill paid out the rope reliably as the initial chimney passed without incident. After about thirty feet one encounters the crux of the climb, a short and smooth slab which, when dry, presents no problems. Today, however, it was wringing wet and dripping with a green carpet of dank lichen, moss and algae. Initial probings confirmed the ice-like properties of the slab and it was only after some serious abuse from Bill that I plucked up the courage to leap for a good handhold several feet higher. Abandoning all pretence of good technique (I was now out of sight of those below so it didn't really matter anyway), I grovelled onto a stately ledge, from where I could clearly see across to the terrified youth who was cowering on a small, sloping heathery ledge. I offered him a few words of encouragement. 'Have you down in no time. Just relax and don't try and move until we get to you.' His position was undoubtedly both precarious and serious and he told me he had already fallen from a ledge ten to twelve feet above. Any further slips would result in certain death.

To reach him involved traversing across an overhanging, slime-covered wall, whose handholds were good, but appeared alarmingly loose and whose footholds were non-existent. Omitting to reveal that I was probably more scared than he was, I launched out across the creaking handholds, only to beat a hasty retreat as one hold moved several inches once weighted. Ready to risk a fall, I set off again, but this time, half way across was relieved to find a familiar face peering out of the gloom above me – the party approaching from the top had managed to descend far enough to make contact, and an alarmingly thin orange rope snaked its way down to me. Clipping this instinctively to my harness, I stepped out above the void with renewed confidence and completed the traverse, trying to appear as composed as possible so as not to further frighten the youth, who was now just a few feet below us. I then found out that the welcome rope from above hadn't in fact been tied to anything at all – it offered merely what climbers call psychological protection!

Three of us were now in a position to organise the rescue and for once it ran perfectly, probably a reflection of the fact that considerably more than three rescuers are normally trying to organise things. Colyn and I quickly arranged anchor points and ropes, Martin Scrowston uttered the appropriate calming noises, and was then lowered down with a spare harness which he clamped tightly around the youth. Both rescuer and casualty were then linked to the same rope, which was controlled by me from above. This was probably the hardest part of the ordeal for the poor lad. If he thought being stuck on the ledge was terrifying, now he was about to be launched off his perch and lowered a full rope-length to the comparative safety of Jack's Rake. Screaming with terror, he was coaxed into leaning out over the misty precipice and, as I let the rope out, he and Martin disappeared into the gloomy evening to touch down a couple of minutes later on what must have seemed palatial ledges on the Rake. I abseiled from the ledge to join them and assisted with a rapid evacuation to the RAF Sea King helicopter which had waited like an overgrown angry bee down by the tarn.

Colyn meanwhile was having to fight his own battle high on Pavey Ark. As he used the fixed ropes to re-ascend the 300 feet back to the top of the crag, another over-enthusiastic team member was removing the main anchor points at the same time! This mix of climber and non-climber, expert and non-expert, can be very useful in straightforward situations, but when high levels of technical skills are involved, it is a dangerous and potentially lethal cocktail.

As the team regrouped, the obvious question had to be asked. What was a young lad (who should have been at school) with no climbing or walking experience, no mountain equipment and only an old pair of trainers for footwear, doing half way up the vast cliffs of Pavey Ark? The answer was as simple as it was unbeliev-able. He had tried to climb the cliff for a £1 bet with his brother on their first visit to the hills. It was almost his last.

The Abraham Club dinner that night proved as exhaustively entertaining as usual. The guest speaker was summarily belittled before delivering a fine speech, the hotel sold more ale than it had done in the whole of the previous week and, as the evening progressed, the stories became taller and the laughter louder. An evening to remember.

At 8 am the next morning I awoke in a daze to the *Mastermind* sound – or so I thought until I realised sod's law was again coming into play and the call-out bleeper was to blame for the early morning intrusion. What could be wrong? Early morning call-outs were almost invariably due to walkers being lost overnight, it being too early for most folk to have departed for the fells that morning. Expecting the news to come over the radio that we were going to have to trek up Rossett Ghyll to Angle Tarn to bring down a group of youngsters whose leaders should never have allowed them to camp there in the first place, it came as a shock to hear the words climber and Raven Crag crackle out of the set. Who on earth would be climbing at this time in the morning? With singularly depressing alacrity, and with a hollow feel in the pit of my stomach, I suddenly realised that there was more than a good chance that the incident involved someone from the previous night's cel-ebrations. Raven Crag was immediately above the hotel, where it was usual for many of the revellers to stay.

Driving down the valley I felt subdued and worried. Was it a fall from the crag, a slip on the path, an illness? Who was it? Was

14

it due to drink or drugs? A broken ankle or arm – or worse? Pulling up at the Old Dungeon I quickly spotted a gathering of bleary-eyed remnants from the previous night's dinner. Their expressions were blank, glazed and sombre.

'It's Dave Seddon – he's come off,' said one. A simple statement with an unstated outcome.

I hurried past, desperate to lend a hand in some way, but most of the gear had already gone. The steep path to the crag passed almost unnoticed and I soon encountered a group of rescuers at the foot of Original Route. Their actions and expressions said everything, words could have added nothing. Dave lay utterly motionless at the foot of the crag. We carried him gently back down to our base at the Old Dungeon Ghyll, where our own team Reverend, Graham Hartley, conducted a short but compassionate and emotional service. Heads bowed and cheeks damp, we slipped away one by one.

No one will ever know the reason for Dave's fall, or indeed know from where he fell. It was an accident in the purest sense of the word. He was a skilled climber of mature judgement and great courage, and he was climbing on routes well within his capabilities. Perhaps a foot- or handhold snapped, or a rock boot slipped on a greasy hold. We'll never know. But, as always, solo-climbing can punish in the most cruel and ruthless way.

After the event, the most striking point for me was the irony of this twenty-four-hour period. A climber of immense talent and experience falls and dies attempting a climb well within his known limits, whilst another person, with absolutely no experience, attempting something way beyond his limits, falls, lands on a ledge and is rescued without injury. Dave was buried in the churchyard at Chapel Stile, surrounded by the fells he loved, and after the accident, his brother Phil trained to become a member of the team.

Not all rescues are by any means as dramatic or as undeniably tragic as these. Many are simple, almost to the point of being unnecessary and, as in any job, there is a fair share of the mundane.

15

At this stage, it is well worth looking at the way in which mountain rescue is organised, as this will assist in understanding the many and various ways in which rescues described in the book start and develop.

2

A TEXTBOOK CASE

An area such as the Lake District has a number of civilian rescue teams, each of which has a clearly defined area of operation. For example, the Langdale/Ambleside team covers an area of the central Lakes which is reasonably well defined by clear geographical features. The eastern boundary runs northwards from Kirkstone Pass summit, over Red Screes, to Fairfield, then down to Dunmail Raise and up again to Steel Fell, across to High Raise, then to Esk Hause. From this well known Spaghetti Junction of the fells the boundary continues across Esk Pike to ascend the ridge to Bowfell and across the crest of Crinkle Crags, right down to the Three Shire Stone on the summit of Wrynose Pass. Up again to Whetside Edge and down into Little Langdale, where the boundary follows the river all the way back to Ambleside via Skelwith Bridge. Going south from Kirkstone summit, the boundary goes as far as the ridge which divides Troutbeck and Kentmere and comes down to take in the Windermere area and the rounded hills to the south, as far as Gummers How, a popular viewpoint some way down towards Newby Bridge. Not only is it a big area geographically, it is also one of the most heavily visited mountain regions in Britain, lying in the centre of our premier National Park.

Other teams have areas which surround this central hub. Starting in the east, we have the Patterdale team, which covers the main eastern fells – the Helvellyn massif in particular, and which is backed up by the Penrith team which has its own outlying area as well as performing a crucial supporting role. Going south, the Patterdale team's area bounds with that of Kendal, who cover the south-eastern Lake District fells as well as the Shap area and some of the Howgills. Bounding the western edge of the Kendal area is the terrain of the Coniston team who were the first rescue team to be set up in the Lake District. The area immediately around Coniston and the popular walking and climbing areas of Dow Crag, Coniston Old Man and the ridge round to Wetherlam, together with their retaining corries holding the famous Coppermines, provide the majority of their rescue incidents. Continuing in a clockwise direction we come to the splendid western fells, with the major valley centres of Eskdale, Ennerdale, Wasdale and Buttermere. Eskdale has its own team centred on the highly respected Outward Bound School and the Wasdale team, whose area includes the mighty bastions of Gable and the Scafells, must surely have the most demanding terrain of all. The next team around is that centred on Cockermouth which, despite being slightly out of the way, covers some important ground in Buttermere and Ennerdale, including the complex and massive buttresses of Pillar Rock. The Keswick team, busiest along with Ambleside, completes the circle, having to deal with the whole of Borrowdale, as well as Skiddaw and Blencathra. There is one additional team at Kirby Stephen, which has an important support role, and also covers the remote fells nearby.

When a call-out occurs, it is up to the Police to decide in which area the accident has happened, so that the correct team can be called upon to help. In fact, the Police are the only body who can call upon the services of the rescue teams, and any call for assistance goes to them via the 999 procedure. This perhaps has some historical relevance, as the Police were originally involved quite heavily in rescue in certain areas, and still are in parts of

18

Scotland. These days, however, the involvement of the Police in Lake District search and rescue is, as far as I can see, very limited. Many of the local constables would struggle to walk up Loughrigg on a fine day with the wind behind them, though there are a few who are keen fell walkers and climbers. More recently the boot seems to be on the other foot, and the Police are keen to involve the mountain rescue teams as much as possible and as early as possible whenever anyone is missing or overdue, and rescue teams do much of the legwork which some years ago would have been Police business.

So, what do you do when you are involved in a mountain accident? Obviously each circumstance is different, and the detailed reaction of those involved will depend upon the numbers present, their abilities and fitness etc. Let's take an example of a group of four walkers at Easedale Tarn, one of whom slips and breaks an ankle. Several things need to happen concurrently. First and foremost, it is important to ensure that no one else gets injured. Although perhaps not a crucial point in our example, if the accident had occurred on steep ground, in an avalanche-prone area or perhaps in a rock climbing environment, it would be a vital initial consideration. Secondly, first aid has to be given to the injured person. What you can realistically do depends upon the nature of the injuries and the skills and equipment available within the group, but if you view first aid as doing the best you can, until more experienced help becomes available, you won't go far wrong. Even if the limit of the group's ability is to keep the casualty warm, comfortable and in good spirits, it is well worth doing and can avoid complications in the rescue at a later stage.

In our example, unless you have advanced first aid training, a broken ankle is best dealt with as follows. Firstly you immobilise the injury in the most comfortable position you can achieve, reducing the chances of further injuries internally, and reducing the pain. Alongside this, you might want to use clothing and equipment to pad beneath the legs for support or to provide insulation from the ground. After this, about all you can do is to provide as much shelter and psychological support as possible, and ensure that the location is made as obvious as possible for the rescue team to locate – especially if visibility is poor. Any unskilled attempts to move the casualty could result in causing further injury, so unless there is a very real threat of stonefall or avalanche, for example, leave the sufferer be.

By contrast, if the ankle is broken so badly that a bone has pierced the skin, an open or compound fracture as it is known, some more advanced first aid is a priority, and the wound has to be padded to prevent bleeding, and enclosed gently to keep dirt out, whilst avoiding pressure on the area of puncture.

Whatever first aid turns out to be necessary, a third major task has to be taking place at the same time, organising one or more group members to get to the nearest telephone, with details of the casualty's injuries and location. If the group has a first aid kit containing a casualty card, or some other means of recording information, they should take this with them so that the essential details are not lost or misinterpreted. The rescuers need to know as much relevant information as possible, and after detailing this to the Police via the 999 call, the informants should wait at the place from where they have phoned until the rescue team arrive and interview them. This is vital, as it can eliminate doubt about locations or injuries, and can assist in a speedier and more efficient evacuation.

The ideal information to have ready for your phone call consists of an accurate grid reference, along with details of any striking visual features of relevance, place names etc, plus the casualty's name and age, and as many details as possible about the injuries. (If in doubt a sprained ankle should be a broken one!) It is worth noting the importance of getting to the nearest telephone as quickly as possible. Trying to raise the alarm at a Mountain Rescue Post as identified on the OS map is likely to be fruitless, as rescue bases are generally unmanned. Some years ago, after an incident in foul conditions above Patterdale, an informant managed to reach the valley and passed several farms and houses with telephones before arriving at the marked Rescue Post which was found deserted. Calling from the phone in the first house passed might have saved the life of the casualty.

The first house to be encountered on the descent from Easedale Tarn is Brimmer Head Farm, and this is where our imaginary informant should have made for. After dodging past the sharp incisors of the farm dogs, and the even sharper fangs of the farmer, Philip Powell, dialling 999 is the next step, although this would be complicated by the terrier which by now would have its mouth firmly wrapped around our informant's ankle. Asking the emergency services operator for Mountain Rescue puts their message directly to the Police, who examine the location of the incident before calling out the appropriate team, in this case the Langdale/Ambleside. As soon as this is decided, Police headquarters in Kendal simply push a button on the phone which activates the call-out procedure. Team members' bleepers bleep or discreetly vibrate, depending on where they are being worn and how much of an effect the wearer wants to have on the company he or she is keeping at the time. More recent radiopagers are also able to display incident details. And a light is brightly illuminated outside the base.

Whoever reaches base first will rush into the control room and press a button on the phone which puts them straight through to Police headquarters who will relay the information which has come from the informant. This is then relayed to other team members via the radio and, in our case, it would go something like this: 'All Langdale Mobiles. All Langdale Mobiles. Call-Out. Call-Out. Broken Ankle at Easedale Tarn. Rendezvous at Brimmer Head Farm.'

By now the first Land Rover will be speeding from Ambleside base, siren blaring and scaring the living daylights out of the tourists, both pedestrian and vehicle-bound, whilst other team members would be making their own way to the incident, headlights full on and with inadequate Mountain Rescue stickers failing to ease progress past the painfully slow tourist traffic. One team member stays at the base to man the radio and ensure effective communication at this early and important stage in the rescue. It is normal for whichever team member lives near the rendezvous point to arrive there before the first Land Rover. They interview the informant thoroughly, until they are satisfied that they have sufficient information about the location of the casualty and the nature of the injuries. This information is relayed to all other team members via the radio, and as soon as the Land Rover arrives, the rescue really gets under way.

Equipment is carried up in order of priority, and the fastest members set off carrying the pacman sac, Entonox and a group shelter, if required. The pacman sac holds all the vital gear which those first on the scene will require, and the contents have undergone modifications over the years to refine the concept. Most important of all is the first aid kit, which contains a variety of drugs, bandages, splints and tape with which the situation can be stabilised. Additional gear includes a radio, light waterproofs, gloves, duvet jacket, hat, map, compass, whistle, flares – some of which may be used for members of the injured party as well as for the rescuers. Other equipment, such as the stretcher, additional specialist first aid gear, spare Entonox and so on, is carried up by the next wave of rescuers and spare bodies walk up to assist with the carry down.

It ought to have taken between five and ten minutes between the 999 call being made from Brimmer Head and the first Land Rover leaving the base, which is a pretty fast response time for a voluntary organisation. The first team member could be interviewing the informant between ten and fifteen minutes after the call, and the fastest team members could be with the casualty just twenty minutes later.

A rapport is quickly established with the casualty. Names are exchanged, some pleasantries, and an explanation of what is going to happen. Questions are asked as to how the accident and injury occurred, where it hurts, is it feeling better, or worse. Before any hands-on first aid is attempted, the casualty is offered something to take the pain away, in this case, most likely some Entonox – Nitrous Oxide or laughing gas, as it may otherwise be known. Several deep draughts on this 'happy gas', a few minutes for the pain to ease, and the casualty's psychological condition can improve dramatically, sometimes to such an extent that it makes the rescuers fall about laughing too. Once the injury becomes pain-free, we remove or cut away trousers and socks and gently ease off the boot, so that we can see the full extent of the injury. This is vital if the treatment is to be accurate. Most ankle fractures exhibit some bruising and potentially severe deformation of the joint but, unless the skin is broken, there's not much the rescuers can do other than immobilise the joint securely, using a soft, flexible Kramer splint, padding and elasticated bandages.

Whilst the first aid is being carried out, the Bell stretcher will have arrived in two parts and been assembled. The large, water-proof and snug 'cas bag' in which the casualty is wrapped will be laid out ready, and as soon as the casualty is ready to move, they will be gently lifted aboard and strapped securely in ready for the carry down.

A team of eight carries the stretcher at any one time. The first and last person wear a rucsac frame, to which the forward and rear extending handles of the stretcher are fastened. Three others line up down each side, each using a long sling attached to the stretcher frame which is wrapped over the shoulder to assist with the carry. The team needs to change over periodically as carrying is hard work, especially on rough ground and on the occasions when the casualty is on the large side (twenty stones is, I think, the record for the Langdale team), plenty of fresh helpers may be required over a long descent.

The carry down from Easedale Tarn takes about thirty-five to forty minutes, and ends in the farmyard at Brimmer Head, un-ceremoniously amongst the sheep muck, farm machinery and abandoned rescue vehicles. An ambulance would have been called earlier and the casualty is carefully lifted from the team's metallic, rough-looking Bell stretcher onto the neat, hospital-style device carried in the ambulance. Family or friends are sorted out with lifts in the ambulance, or with us to pick up their own vehicles and, after some friendly banter, the whole circus turns round in the farmyard, cuts up a bit more of Philip's grass and departs. The ambulance will head to the new Westmorland Hospital in Kendal (about thirty-five minutes' drive), team members will drift reluctantly back to work, if they are employed by others, or if self-employed may display considerably more alacrity. Those with a noble heart, forgiving employers or bugger all else to do may end up back at the base, brewing up, replacing gear and preparing for the next time.

In a perfect world such rescue incidents are easily and quickly dealt with but, inevitably, there are times when things just don't go according to plan. Right at the very start of the rescue, when the informant telephones for help is the first potential pitfall. For incidents close to the road, the ambulance service may get called out instead, and there have been several times when an ambulance has been despatched to an accident, only to find that the casualty is just a little far from the road, and the ground just a little too rough for the two paramedics to cope with the carry. I've often wondered why this should happen. Perhaps there is a little bit of inter-emergency service competition, or perhaps the informant's description of the location is too vague. Whatever the case, there is always a further delay for the casualty as the team are called out to assist.

Grid references can be a problem for some folk. All this 'along the corridor and up the stairs' nonsense, Eastings and Northings, six figure and eight figure references, why it's enough to confuse anyone. Well, not really it isn't, in fact being able to take an accurate grid reference is a fundamental and crucial aspect of basic navigational skills, and explained in words of one syllable on every OS map, yet folk do get things the wrong way round. Many years ago, when Spider Penman was team leader we had a call-out in Langdale to a grid reference which translated to Sheep Crag near

Silver Howe. Not a popular place Sheep Crag, so the informant was quizzed further and the casualty was found to be several miles away near Pavey Ark, the result of the informant having absolutely no idea of how to read a map or take a grid reference. Another incident I recall had a grid reference somewhere in the Irish Sea, which I assumed was incorrect as there aren't too many mountains there.

Once on the hill, poor communication or unreliable information can be extremely confusing. Attending a rescue at the top of Easy Gully on Pavey Ark, a group of rescuers, including myself and Spider, were scrambling urgently up the gully at the same time that the stretcher and casualty were being carried down the easy ground round to the side and out of sight. Having found no sign of any injured walkers or indeed of the rest of the rescue team, we rather sheepishly regained contact by radio to find the casualty was well on the way down to Stickle Tarn.

Nowadays one could be forgiven for thinking that modern communication methods would have all but eliminated mistakes and made the whole rescue process more reliable, quicker and safer. To a point, this is true. The use of radiopagers and more efficient radio systems has helped, as has the availability of very specialist kit such as portable faxes. And then there are mobile phones. As these wretched devices have become cheaper and increasingly efficient both in terms of the area they serve and the length of time they can be left on, more and more fell walkers are carrying them. I've heard all the excuses: 'It's only for emergencies.' 'I never use it when I'm walking.' 'It's a good safety feature.' At first glance, much of this makes good sense. The time saved if a rescue team can be called out by mobile phone is quite consider-able, and a direct line is then established with the accident site through which ongoing advice and instructions can be given, and up-to-date information received. Recent experiences, however, have shown that this is only one side of the story.

The burly leader of the Langdale/Ambleside team, Stewart Hulse, has his own delicate way of broaching the topic. He describes calls for help which have been made through mobiles as 'wipe-my-backside-calls', continuing, 'We already pack two rolls of Andrex for people like them.' And that's not all. He accuses them of 'becoming a scourge', and in the team's 1994 report, Mr Hulse suggests a new award – 'The Queen Mother's Fearless 40's Award for Feckless and Farcical Fellwalkers', and he adds, 'Some Mr or Mrs Bean could soon be asking for crumpets and Bovril to be brought up if they feel peckish ... Use it for real emergencies or placing a bet with the bookie's,' continues Stewart, revealing his main weakness in life. He's certainly got a way with words!

Forgetting the issue of mobile phones for a moment, here's another gem from Stewart, commenting this time on European legislation requiring rescue teams to prove their innocence in the event of a claim being made against them, rather than the claimant having to prove their negligence: 'I think they have a man locked up in a box in Brussels, and every so often they let him out of the box and hit him over the head until he comes up with something daft.' And I thought we were simply up against an over-bureaucratic European parliament with little understanding of national and localised issues. Maybe Stewart has also inadvertently hit on the government's secret decision-making process.

Back to mobile phones. The first call-out I can remember involving a mobile phone was in Langdale, when a group of walkers were making an ascent of the Langdale Pikes from Stickle Tarn. The day was cold, with some heavy snow showers temporarily obscuring visibility and dusting the ground white. Once the bad weather hit the group, one would have thought that with the limited skills and equipment they had available, the sensible option would have been to retrace their steps. Obviously that was too simple, and they continued a short way before deciding that the lack of visibility and their lack of knowledge had rendered them lost. Had they not had a mobile phone with them, they would have had to extricate themselves from their predicament, which I am sure would have been quite easy, had they had the presence of mind to think clearly and use what little common sense they appeared to possess. But no, the mobile phone was there in the rucsac and what an easy option it offered. A quick call to the rescue services, who would be able to tell them the way down, would solve the problem. There was one major flaw with this strategy, which was that the group did not know their location, and as you might imagine, it's not easy giving a description of how to descend from a completely unknown location, apart from the obvious – 'Walk downhill!'

Some detailed questioning of the group revealed that they were in fact somewhere above Stickle Tarn, and they were told to progress steadily down the obvious path, following the equally obvious cairns, whilst a couple of rescuers went to ensure their safety. They were found, cold and disorientated just a short way from Stickle Tarn. Thus, the double edge of the mobile phone's sword is revealed. However well-intentioned the owner may be, the phone is always there, burning a hole in the rucsac, screaming to be used and providing the softest of soft options.

Other similar incidents have followed and, though the use of mobile phones can sometimes be a real help, members of the public cannot always be trusted to make the right judgements as to when this time might be. As their ownership and use become even more widespread, call-outs by mobile phone could change mountain rescue work significantly, and increase the workload on already overstretched resources. The other factors which come into play here are the psychological and aesthetic overtones which mirror much of modern life. Mountain walking and climbing have always provided a chance to take time out from the pressures of everyday life, a chance to escape the bureaucracy and technology which threaten to strangle our expression and individuality. Mountain-eering is about many things, for example self-reliance and experi-encing nature in the raw, making your own decisions and minimising the risks with your own experience and skills. In ten years time I suppose most hill walkers will be carrying mobile phones and GPS navigational systems as well. If so, I just hope they will have the sense to use these as valuable additions to their traditional skills of judgement, map-reading and self-reliance, and not as a replacement, otherwise I can see mountain rescue teams having to have desk-bound personnel doing nothing but offering advice by phone to walkers who know where they are but don't know how to get to where they want to be! An unrealistic proposition? Wait and see!

The last word on this, which should also serve as a warning to all, concerns a family group who were on holiday in Langdale. The parents decided to partake of a fine lunch in the valley, and sent the kids off for a short walk armed with a mobile phone and the instructions that they should call 999 if they had any problems. You can imagine the rest! So, learn to navigate, get the weather forecast before you set out, equip yourself well and leave that mobile phone at home!

3

IT WAS A DARK
AND STORMY NIGHT

So many mountain rescues take place in foul weather, yet for me, natural phenomena hold an eternal and enthralling fascination. Every extreme, from flood to frost and from heatwave to hurricane, carries with it an effect on the landscape, the environment and our senses which captures the imagination of most outdoor enthusiasts. Of all the personal memories I recall best, those involving extremes of weather are as frequent as any. I can clearly remember peering out of my school windows into a stormcloud so dense that for a time day turned to night in an underworld-like vision. Minutes later, hail stones as big as golf balls rained down like flak, denting cars, smashing windows, turning a summer's day white, and reducing my father's crop of potatoes and barley to a premature stubble. I can remember the whirlwind that tossed hay a couple of hundred feet into the air on an otherwise sultry afternoon, and the violent winds which lifted our barn roof clean off in one piece and dumped it a hundred yards away in the stackyard. And then there are Michael Fish's famous last words on hurricanes. For most of us, the weather remains one of the last vestiges of the natural world which still exerts a major and genuinely tangible influence on us. We don't normally fear attack from wild beasts or have to prepare for days away from home, hunting in a dangerous environment, yet we can really feel the cold or the heat, we struggle to steer our cars on snowbound tarmac, and we shiver at the blast of an icy wind or nearby lightning strike.

For those operating in mountain environments, the weather dominates everything, from the way we plan our days to the sights we see. Weather watching becomes a severely problematic addiction, with the BBC weather bulletins at 6.30 or 9.30 compulsive viewing, along with habitual flicking through the Ceefax reports from the Scottish ski areas to try and catch any subtle changes in the predicted patterns which might influence the following hours or days. We read books on weather prediction to understand a little more clearly the complex patterns and interactions which affect our mountain areas, and we study a variety of reports and long term assessments, along with reflections on past records. With some of the biggest computers in the world helping predict pressure changes and resultant weather patterns, and with so much literature and information available from telephone services, the Internet and the Met Office, you would be forgiven for thinking that reasonably accurate predictions would now be possible. You would of course be completely and utterly wrong.

In mountain areas especially, the weather is not just a series of transient phases which arise from the positions of low and high pressures, cold and warm fronts. No, the mountains create their own weather, and exert considerable influence. Weather fronts drag as they pass by, leaving bad weather in mountains for longer periods. Mountain slopes force air currents upwards, leading to rapid cloud formation and frequent precipitation. A variety of unpredictable micro climates are readily produced, and the only sure prediction is unpredictability. All those computers and all the best dressed and most eloquent weather persons in the world won't change the fact that the natural elements will always (thankfully) retain a major element of uncertainty.

The weather and mountain accidents are inextricably linked. Very wet spells produce saturated and extremely slippery ground, which can lead to a spate of 'broke-ankle slipping on wet grass/ rock'-type incidents. Heavy snowfall can create serious avalanche problems, especially when accompanied by strong winds, which even by themselves can blow walkers or climbers over hard enough to cause injury. Prolonged hard weather brings ice and extensive snow cover which will always catch the unwary on places such as the Helvellyn edges and hot sunshine can produce cases of heat stroke or heat exhaustion. And then there are storms.

I have always been totally hooked on, yet deeply suspicious of, mountain storms. One of my greatest fears in the mountains has always been of a lightning strike, and stories of great Alpine ascents in which storms rage around those involved, with lightning blasting boulder-like shrapnel from the mother rock, and some-times climbers too, did nothing to alleviate these fears. I then learnt of a climber who worked for the National Trust, Neil Allinson, who was also a mountain guide, who had apparently been struck. The accident was said to have happened on the North Face of the Piz Badile, a huge shovel-shaped peak, famous for its soaring granite walls and ridges and notorious for sudden weather changes and violent storms. Stranded on the famous Cassin Route on the North Face, the storm exploded around him, and as the lightning struck Neil repeatedly, he had nowhere to go. Miraculously, he survived, and though there were rumours that the accident turned his hair white and changed his personality, I always found Neil an affable, open and genuinely enthusiastic character, with a deep love of mountains and mountaineering, though every time I looked at his fine mane of white hair I was reminded of the terrifying story.

Several years later I sat on the campsite beneath the Piz Badile, contemplating the same incident and planning an ascent of the classic, though easier, North Ridge. It's a long walk from the valley bottom to the hut beneath the ridge, and still an hour's slog to the foot of the climb, which is at a narrow neck on the ridge itself at the start of the difficulties. Wanting to solo the climb, I opted for a bivouac at the foot of the ridge, hoping to avoid the congestion which is common as parties staying at the hut arrive en masse. The conditions did not look too bad on the approach walk, but as I neared the base of the ridge just before dusk, a low rumble confirmed the presence of a nearby storm. Quickly establishing the most suitable site, and preparing Karrimat and bivvy bag, I sat hunched up, gazing at the darkening skies and listening to the menacing growl of the storm which was steadily encroaching closer to the Badile. The first flashes of lightning were vague and distant, but as the storm grew in rage, so the streaks of white and blue grew closer and the grumbling louder. The storm did not strike with a sudden vengeful fury, but grew steadily until the first huge raindrops spattered on the flimsy, inadequate nylon of the bivvy bag, which before the trip had seemed so reliable. Within a few minutes, the feat of staying dry went from improbable to impossible, and the storm was all around me.

The only option was to stay put and sit it out, for retreat in the dark would have been most unpleasant. Between bouts optimistically described as fitful dozing, I lay and thought of Neil's hair. In the equally optimistically described grey light of dawn, I retreated down cold slabs which streamed with water to face an eternally long and dreadfully wet descent back to the valley. When I got down, I went straight to the campsite bathroom and checked in the mirror. My hair had not turned white. Two days later I sat on the same ledge in a similar storm (I really must get a grip on these Italian weather forecasts), but awoke to a stunning, clear dawn which heralded a marvellous day and a successful ascent of the route.

The reality of a lightning strike came harshly to me in the summer of 1985. Following a long, phenomenally hot and sultry spell of weather, a storm was as inevitable as it was that the sun would set. The humidity was extraordinary and as the day decayed into its rumbustious finale, I sought shelter at Brimmer Head Farm, below Easedale valley. The rain was copious, instantly drenching and accompanied by the strong winds which are created as a result of the strength of the rising air current in the centre of such a big

32

cumulo-nimbus as this. Even the dogs had managed to creep indoors. Lightning strikes were making the external telephone bell at the farm ring sharply and on occasions the phone itself twittered and jingled. Then, the knock on the door 'Can I use your telephone – there's been an accident.' A sodden character squelched into the kitchen to relate the incident. There had been a lightning strike on the Easedale Tarn path and someone was clearly in a bad way. Leaving the rest of them to take the risk of dealing with the humming telephone and to contact the emergency services, I headed off to the casualty who was about half a mile away. Although it still rained heavily, the storm was passing over and the air felt fresh and cool.

Though pleasant, this did little to stem the flow of thoughts racing through my mind. I had never had to deal with a lightning strike before and had absolutely no idea what to expect. I was afraid that I would arrive on the scene and be unsure what to do, be incapable of dealing with the situation. I jogged up the track, remembering as always to walk the last section to the casualty site so as not to appear too out of breath, a ploy which never seemed to work for me anyway. I arrived at a small group of walkers, huddled glumly together by the wall, a hundred yards or so up the track. Across the path, a short distance away lay the body of a man. One of the group came forward, a nurse, who had been trying to revive him for almost half an hour without success. After a short discussion, we persuaded those not directly involved to head away from the accident scene so as to attract as little attention to it as possible, and we encouraged the dead man's family to walk down to the farm.

When the story behind the incident unfolded it was as bizarre as it was tragic. The family had been to Easedale Tarn fishing, and on the descent had run into the storm. They took refuge beneath a tall larch tree on the edge of the path and sat there to wait for the storm to pass. The man had been sitting on his haunches beneath the tree, holding the fishing rod up, like an aerial, at the same time. When the lightning struck, it sent its terrible shock down the tree and earthed partially through the group sitting there, injuring two members and killing the man instantly. The tree still bears the scars of the strike, its top twenty feet or so now completely lifeless. The power of the strike must have been formidable. Each ring on the fishing rod was incomplete, melted apart like a burnt out piece of fuse wire. The blue nylon cagoule which the victim had been wearing could only be described as shredded. Tiny strips of material lay around on the damp ground and it would have been impossible to guess how the damage could have been caused had one not known. The body was scorched with the force of the strike, his feet and chest in particular bearing the brunt of the power, probably indicating where the lightning struck and earthed.

This was the first time I had been first on the scene at a fatality and it was quite a disturbing few minutes which I spent alone with the man before the rest of the team arrived. Most rescuers deal with mountain fatalities in a similar way I suspect, in that the emotion of the situation is kept firmly locked away, and you just try not to get involved in the human side of things beyond the professional retrieval of the body and the provision of as much care as possible for others who may have been present. Yes, it's sad, unbelievably cruel sometimes, but I suspect that if we thought about it too much, we would probably give up mountaineering ourselves and take up something more secure, like chess.

Lightning strikes have killed since. In 1988, I was climbing on Scafell with Bill Birkett and Wilf Williamson when a storm crept over so gently we observed little change in the conditions until the first deep rumble of thunder reverberated around the crags. As we hurried off the top of the East Buttress, a bolt of lightning struck the crag close to the descent route known as Broad Stand, bursting stone from stone and sending a shower of debris over the cliff edge. You have probably come across the phrase 'adrenaline rush', well we had one! As the storm drifted over the Lake District fells, it left behind it a trail of disaster. Near the outflow of Red Tarn below Catstycam, two men and a woman were struck by lightning, killing one of the men and leaving the other two suffering from burns and shock. Simultaneously, on the ridge of Greatrigg Man, part of the popular Fairfield Horseshoe, a group of four walkers were also struck. One man was killed and the other three suffered from minor injuries, burns and shock. Both incidents were dealt with by the local rescue teams, backed up by a helicopter from RAF Boulmer.

Storms are not uncommon on the British mountains, so what should you do if you get caught in one? The first and most obvious statement is that if at all possible, you should avoid walking or climbing in any exposed places if storms have been forecast or look likely. You should avoid exposed summits or ridges and flat open spaces, and in no circumstances should you take shelter beneath a tree. If you are in an exposed place, but with a little time before the storm reaches you, you should attempt to descend as quickly as possible, aiming for any area in which there are plenty of objects higher than you, like boulderfields or undulating scree slopes. Keep low and do not put yourself in a position where you may be the highest or even one of the highest points nearby. Keep away from vertical rock or isolated boulders – at least the same distance away as the height of the feature. Avoid cracks in the ground or beneath cliffs as they can transfer a ground current. Also avoid cave entrances, or overhangs of rock, across which the current can arc. The position you adopt on the ground should be as tight as possible, crouching or sitting with the knees raised for example. Insulate yourself from the ground with whatever you have to hand, rubber-soled boots, rucsacs, clothing (preferably as dry as possible), and you should always avoid direct contact with any rock feature – sit away from rather than lean against a crag. The presence of metal objects apparently adds little or nothing to the electrical danger, the climber's body being a more attractive target as it is higher and offers less resistance.

We were caught out by a completely unexpected storm last summer on a ridge in Austria's Dachstein Alps. Generally poor visibility and the proximity of the surrounding peaks prevented any possibility of prior knowledge of the storm's approach; once again the menacing growl of thunder being the first indication of trouble. We were on a knife-edge ridge at the time, following a series of steel cables, ladders and spikes that had been placed to make the going easier, and at that point, descent to the sides was impossible – we would have to climb a 200-foot step in the ridge ahead before we could access an easier route off. There followed a near panic-stricken race up the engineered bars and steps which forged a route up the steep sidewall, but this was still almost vertical, and hard work. Once on the crest of the ridge, we jogged along terrain which would normally have demanded more care, and careered down some steep screes to join a party of fifteen or so ahead of us who were also deserting the ridge at high speed. It was interesting to note the effects of the approaching storm on the metal cables which festoon the ridge. They buzzed with static, and on several occasions my companions Johannes and Paul yelped with surprise as they received minor shocks through the wire. No one was injured, but the unscheduled descent gave us an extra few hours' walking to reach the valley – a fair exchange for our safety.

Violent winds are a common feature of mountain weather, and there are several common causes. Firstly, the wind can be strong everywhere, conditions usually found when deep areas of low pressure cross the country, and in these situations winds will be considerably stronger throughout upland areas. Secondly, localised landscape shapes can have a profound effect on wind speeds and directions. Classically, the tops of ridges and slopes attract severe winds, as the air flow which is hitting the side of the slope has to escape upwards towards the top of the hillside. As it does, it is compressed to join existing high-level winds flowing at ridge top level. This gives wind speeds which can be two or three times higher or more than those just a short way down the slope. Another important result of certain land shapes is the funnelling effect which forces air currents through gaps in the mountains commonly known as cols. In this case, in addition to the wind being compressed upwards, it is compressed laterally, to funnel through the line of least resistance. Classical examples of this are Windy Gap below Great and Green Gable, and Three Tarns between Crinkle Crags and Bowfell. Other more localised effects can be problematic. Wind speeds can increase many times during the summer months when strong thermals – bubbles of heated air – are active. The effect called rotoring can also create strong, blustery conditions in the lee of ridges, when the wind direction can be directly opposite that which one would expect.

However the strong winds we encounter are created, their effect is the same. Gusts can blow us over, sweep us off our feet, impede progress, push us off our required bearing and effectively lower the temperature we feel – an effect known as wind-chill. Different forecasts may use different terminology. Some will give wind strengths in miles per hour, others in that mystical figure, metres per second (How many readers know what a 5 m/s wind feels like?). Some, such as the shipping forecasts, stick strictly to the Beaufort Scale which describes the force of the wind eg: gale force 8, and others just use fresh, strong, gale, severe gale, etc. Problems on the mountains usually start with lower level wind speeds of fresh to strong (forces 5–7 or speeds 19–32 mph). At higher levels, these winds are likely to be strong to gale, or even severe gale in exposed locations. If wind speeds reach gale force at low levels, they could be storm force on the mountains, making progress impossible. As a general guide, gale force winds (force 8–9) make the going extremely tough, whilst severe gale and storm force winds (10–12) render conditions so severe that not only is progress severely impeded, but gusts can fell us with unbelievable speed and power. A quick look at the accident stastics for 1988 in the Lake District demonstrates the effect of winds on mountain safety. Out of a total of thirty accidents between the beginning of the year and the 6th March, six occurred as a direct result of wind power. One man received fatal injuries when he was blown from a ridge onto scree and another was blown onto a cornice which collapsed above Brown Cove, Helvellyn. Another man died in a similar location after strong winds blew him off a ridge, whilst two others slipped after being blown over, receiving relatively minor injuries.

The final incident involved a man who was blown from the top of Red Ghyll, Scafell, resulting in a fall of about 600 feet and serious injuries.

Strong mountain winds are not a problem for everyone and for some they are positively welcome. One of the rather offbeat sports which I and several other enthusiasts in the Lake District enjoy is Upskiing – sailing on skis with the aid of a very large, parachute-shaped canopy. In stronger winds the canopy produces enough power to pull a skier up any gradient, or sail fast and furious along undulating ground. The very nature of the sport and the sometimes venomous power of the winds makes this a potentially dangerous activity, as a couple of people have found out. I once went to the ski slopes of Glenshee to demonstrate Upskiing to Gustav Fischnaller, a leading ski instructor and hang glider pilot. He was extremely keen to give it a try, but as he was teaching skiing for most of the day, we had to wait until the end of the lessons before we could get together. I had found a good location between two pistes, with a wind rushing right up the slope, though it was gusting to about 40 mph at the top of the slope and caution was the keynote. Once Gustav was free, I gave him some instructions, clipped a spare canopy to his harness and we enjoyed several thrilling uphill runs, at speeds well in excess of those which most recreational downhillers would be comfortable with. Gustav then made an error which could have cost him his life.

Instead of trailing the canopy behind him, which allows the wind to keep the lines in the top of the venting device free, he gathered it up in a huge bundle to reduce the drag and skied down. On his next ascent, I observed him disappearing beyond the extent of the slope which had been our far point and, for a brief instant, saw a ski fly up sideways. That something had gone wrong was clear, but it was not until I arrived at the top of the slope that I found out just what. I vented my canopy, spilling the wind and rendering the fifty-five square metres of sail impotent near the point at which the hill rounded off towards its summit, and then followed Gustav's ski tracks on foot. I came across one ski first, then another, then blood. Then more blood, spattered on rocks and spreading in the snow. By now, I was on the lee side of the hill, and there was still no sign of him. Following the trail in the snow, I descended over steepening ground, to find Gustav sitting upright, delirious and bleeding from a nasty looking head wound. It was virtually dark and at that stage I genuinely feared for his safety. It was a long way back to the ski station to raise help, so after checking him over for other injuries, I wrapped him in the canopy to keep him as warm as possible and started back up the long slope to get my skis.

The snow was deep and only partially consolidated and upwards progress was hard and slow. Shocked by the incident, I felt my legs draining of energy, and each step sank deep into the soft slab. What had happened to the famous adrenaline rush that goes alongside adversity, I wondered grimly. I reached the rounded summit and my skis, clipped into my bindings and set off in the dark, heading down towards the distant lights. Amazingly, just over the first brow I came face to face with the most comforting sight of the day, a sturdy piste basher carrying out his evening duties, heading directly up the hill towards me. Waving and gesticulating, I pulled him over, snapped out of my bindings and gave him the unpleasant details. The driver radioed the information back to the ski patrol centre as he manoeuvred the piste-mashing monster skilfully around exposed granite boulders, some-how grinding out a route into the corrie where Gustav lay. When our lights picked out the colourful material of the Upski canopy flapping in the wind, we headed directly for that location, to find Gustav conscious, but groggy. Other helpers arrived, unseen faces inspiring confidence in the dark with comforting humour and knowledgeable comments. Strong arms loaded Gustav into the back of a piste basher cab, rescuers clung to its sides and it ground its way back through the deep cold of the night to the lights and security offered by the ski centre. I found the whole incident quite harrowing and, for a change, experienced the rescue as an inform-ant and not as a rescuer – a dramatically different sensation I can assure you! Gustav was taken to hospital and detained for a few days, but made a full recovery.

A post-mortem (of the equipment, not Gustav), revealed that the standard release mechanism had jammed due to a small hard ball of snow building up inside a nylon sleeve. The secondary release mechanism which would have ensured his safety had not been operated. This was actually due to too much knowledge on Gustav's part and not too little. After the initial release failed to operate, he attempted to collapse the canopy by pulling in the top risers and forcing the wind to blow down on top of it. This works with paragliders, which he was used to operating, but not necessarily with an Upski. At the end of the day, as in so many other mountain accidents, the cause could be put down to human error.

Of the other elements which pose problems on the hills, mist is one of the most feared by walkers. Low cloud in mountain areas limits visibility and distorts the visible landscape, making tiny outcrops appear as towering crags, and small hummocks as sizeable peaks. As the visibility deteriorates, so does our confidence, and it takes great skill with map and compass to navigate confidently in bad visibility. If you suffer the additional misfortune of being overtaken by darkness, the problem is compounded severely and, without a torch, progress can be impossible. This situation is known as benightment, and it is not to be recommended.

The one and only time I suffered from this unfortunate predicament was in Spain, with not a shred of mist in sight. Inland from Benidorm is the Puig Campana, an impressive limestone peak with a long and classic-looking ridge which falls down to its seaward side. Our aim was to walk up to, and then climb the ridge, which is probably about 1500 feet high. I will miss out the details of getting lost in the half-complete urbanisations beneath the mountain, and of getting lost on the climb and indeed of the initial part of the descent on which we were also lost. Our luck finally changed on the last part of the descent, which was being carried out in an optimistically termed twilight. Our abseils had been slow, but safe, and we reckoned that as the night closed around us, we were just a couple of rope-lengths from the ground at the most. Anchoring the ropes around a stout spiky shrub which sprouted impossibly from the compact limestone, we abseiled free down to a reasonable ledge which measured approximately six feet by three. On descents such as this, the abseil is performed on either a single rope doubled, or more commonly by joining two ropes together, and placing the knot just to one side of the anchor point. Once the descent is complete, pulling the right end of the rope brings the other end sliding down after it, allowing the descent to continue in the same manner.

Back on our ledge, we pulled. The rope slid about twenty feet without a hitch, but suddenly our hearts sank as the rope jammed, unseen somewhere above us. We pulled again, flicked ripples up the rope in the hope of freeing the obstruction, threw it to the left and to the right, pulled again but somehow up there in the darkness, the rope was securely jammed. Trying to climb up was out of the question – the rock was steep and compact, and we were not on a recognised climb. Climbing the rope would have been potentially disastrous – if the snag had suddenly and unexpectedly freed itself, downward progress would have been swift and inevitable. After all, abseiling is only the second fastest way down. So, we stayed put. Tee shirts, shorts and one communal jumper offered little protection against the cool night air, and sleep was at best an optimistic thought. Most frustrating of all was the thought that the lights below looked so close, and offered such promise of cool beer and hot food, yet were as utterly unattainable as a pint of real Tetley bitter in London. Dawn arrived as it always does, not that I see it that often, and the visibility steadily improved until we could see the ground, which lay frustratingly just ten or twelve feet below us and which was easily reached by a short scramble to our left. As if this wasn't sufficiently enraging, we could see the rope dangling from a similarly prickly shrub to the one which we had abseiled from, and one really hard tug sent it spiralling down. At least we made it back to the hotel for breakfast!

Benightments in Britain are common, both due to errors of judgement and to the onset of bad weather and nightfall. Those equipped with torches (spare battery and bulbs of course), and armed with an array of good navigational skills such as pacing, timing and following bearings, may find their way down without problems, and even enjoy the experience. Others may not, as some of the following incidents demonstrate.

If you are determined to get lost, the Lake District is probably not your best place. Other less strikingly featured areas such as the bleak Pennine moorlands would be a better bet. In the Lakes, paths are plentiful and often as heavily cairned as they are eroded. The majority of valleys lead down to farmsteads or minor roads and, except in atrocious conditions, most competent walkers will get off the fells without too much difficulty in bad visibility. There are exceptions. In the Langdale area Crinkle Crags is one of the most deceptive fell tops. The path along the crest of the ridge changes direction frequently to avoid the rockiest knolls and roughest screes, and descent onto the Eskdale side in mistake for the Langdale valley is a common error. Perhaps I ought not admit to this, but it has happened to me a couple of times, on both occasions in the company of those who should have known better. Rumour has it that the taxi service in Eskdale does a roaring trade on bad days, and fears the onslaught of the new breed of GPS units which would make a serious hole in their earnings.

In the winter of 1990, group of friends out walking across Crinkle Crags met atrocious conditions on the summits, with severe gale force winds and terrible visibility. One of their group became separated from the main party and despite frantic efforts to locate him, he remained apart. The group decided to descend, thinking that their estranged member would find his own way down, and meet them later – quite a sensible proposition in the circumstances as he was reasonably experienced. Well, later came and went, and so did later still and the friend failed to show. Weather conditions had deteriorated further still, and severe gale or storm force winds were forecast all night on the fells. After the call for help came, enough team members were dragged screaming from their beds or screaming even more from various hostelries in the area to mount a search for him.

The main problem, apart from the weather, was that the Crinkle Crags ridge is such a vast area, with a good number of paths leading off it, a myriad pattern of sheep trods and countless hollows and small crags which produce a highly complex land form. In order that the area could be searched thoroughly, extra help was required from the search dogs, and from the teams at Kendal and Eskdale, who would approach the area from their side. An operation of this magnitude requires careful planning, along with excellent communication.

The first action has to be to obtain as much information as possible from the informants. We must find out exactly where the lost person was last seen and at what time. What was their experience level, how good was their equipment, did they have spare clothing, a survival bag, how well did they know the area, did they have any medical condition? The questions have to be thorough and the answers as accurate as possible, because the way in which the search is handled will depend on the information available. In this case, the answers given by the missing man's colleagues presented us with a scenario which was worrying. The man was an experienced walker and was well-equipped, but did not have a survival bag. By all accounts, he had sufficient time and skill to have enabled him to descend safely, so the worry was that he had injured himself in some way, or become lost and benighted. Either situation would have been serious due to the atrocious weather conditions. The search had to be organised quickly, and structured in such a way that the most likely scenarios were covered first. Therefore, all the main paths which descend from Crinkle Crags had to be checked, followed by the area in which the missing man was last seen, followed by other possible descents which could prove difficult to negotiate, such as gullies or ghylls. This is relatively easy to arrange in principle, but the hard fact remained that in conditions such as those, it would have been easy to have walked a few yards to the side of the missing man and not see him.

By 11 pm, the search had begun. Small groups of two or three, some with search dogs, set off from Langdale to aim for the man's last known position via different routes. The Band to Three Tarns, Oxendale to Red Tarn, Wrynose summit along to Red Tarn, the Hell Gill path to Three Tarns, the main path from Ling Cove, Eskdale and onto Long Top from the same valley, also into Adam a Cove and Mosedale. Rescuers were then allocated to less obvious descents, such as beneath Shelter Crags onto Whoreneyside Breast, the Cold Pike area, Gaitscale Gill and Crinkle Ghyll, which was my allotted route, along with Dave Till and Peter Farrand. As was the case with many other team members, the sharp gusts of wind and the cold damp air soon cleared my head and the after effects of a few pints were soon dismissed in concentrating on the task in hand.

Crinkle Ghyll is a long jagged gash which rents the fellsides beneath the central, Langdale, side of Crinkle Crags. The approach to it is deceptively long and the upper section alarmingly steep and loose. There have been a number of accidents here, and anyone trying to descend in the dark would have had problems. The ascent of the ghyll actually proved to be quite fun, and we entered into the spirit of the occasion by enjoying our night-time scramble immensely, partially due to the fact that, aware of the summit ridge weather conditions, we knew it would be no fun up there. Our torches picked out daft Herdwicks, stunted trees and rocky blocks and pinnacles, and our voices rang out over the rocky coves when the wind lulled sufficiently to allow it, but we found no trace. The scrambling at the top end of the ghyll is the most difficult section and the quantity of water rushing down the confines of the chasm made it awkward and slippery. I think we were quite glad to exit up the steepening grass slopes above the delta-like head of the beck, but somewhat in awe of what was to come. The wind had strengthened, and in our present position, about 400 feet below the summit ridge, we felt the swirling eddies of the rotor effect from the ridge blast us from all directions.

Our next aim was to scramble up the steep slopes leading to the crest of the ridge and, to make the search more efficient, we decided to split up, and travel approximately one hundred yards apart until we hit the ridge, where we would regroup. At this level, we came across the first snow patches (remarkably insignificant considering it was early February), which consisted of well-thawed granular snow which was just starting to get hard again. I soon lost sight of Pete and Dave completely, and the wind fair shrieked and howled across the ridge, now just a hundred feet or so above me. It was good to be in the company of people who you could trust to look after themselves, undoubtedly a pre-requisite in conditions such as these. Dave was a climber working in the field of outdoor pursuits and management training and, though not exactly a bundle of laughs, he had a well-concealed dry sense of humour and always exerted a calming influence on things. Above all, he was reliable, and I always felt that if there was a job to be done, we could rely on Dave to do it well. Peter was a former colleague from the National Park Ranger Service, a tall and gangly individual who always looked as if he needed a good meal. Though without any sort of background in mountaineering, Peter learnt through his experiences on the Lakeland fells and became a competent fell walker. Steady and reliable, the only problem we might have had with him was getting blown over in the wind, but as we were soon to find out, no one was to be immune from that!

As we reached the rounded rim of the ridge proper, the full violence of the stormy winds struck us hard from the west, and threatened to catapult us back into the corrie from which we had just ascended. Although we were only a hundred yards apart at most, the severe winds and darkness made contact with each other impossible, so I aimed for the path and waited until Dave caught up. It was impossible to stand upright and progress had to be made by crouching low, feet wide apart to increase stability, and even then we were hurled to the ground repeatedly, as if by some mystical and irresistible force. We were on the ridge just south of the notorious Bad Step, which in reality is little more than a ten-foot climb out of a shallow gully, but in these conditions we thought it would live up to its name. Peter had not appeared, and we searched for him for a few minutes, shouting in vain as the wind whipped our words away over the lip of crags and hurled them, unheard, into the valley below. Dave and I clawed our way up the damp rocks on the Bad Step and crawled along the rocky shelf above, taking refuge behind every possible outcrop and boulder to avoid the buffeting gusts which threatened to send us tumbling. Then we saw Peter, leaning at such a seemingly imposs-ible angle into the force of the wind that if the wind died he would have fallen flat on his face.

Talk about huddled conferences! Decisions can be reached so much more quickly in conditions of such adversity and we soon agreed to walk spread out as best we could along the path towards Long Top, keeping within sight of each other's torches and doing what we could to search the area as well as was humanly possible. In fairness, we thought we had virtually no chance whatsoever of finding the missing walker, and it felt as though we were just going through the motions, flashing our feeble torches into the blackness and shouting hopelessly until we were hoarse. It would have been easy to have walked past someone lying just a few yards away, and this fact, combined with the atrocious conditions, gave our search little hope of success. Yet suddenly and utterly unexpec-tedly, the beam of my torch picked out a flash of blue amongst the boulders on Long Top and I redirected the beam to home in on the source. Unbelievably it was the man for whom we searched. He was recumbent on one of the most exposed sections of the ridge, curled around his rucsac and leaning on a few stubby lumps of rock which jutted from the rough pathside. Relieved at finding him, we were doubly relieved to find him alive, and if not exactly well, not exactly unwell either. He was cold, exhausted, wet and, in his own words, 'Bloody glad to see you!' – a sentiment we shared.

Our priority was to move him from the desperately exposed ridge to a more sheltered location, where we could erect a bivouac shelter and check him over before making a decision concerning the evacuation. Dave and I took hold of one arm each, and we led him on a crouching crawl across the rocky plateau, aware that to stand up could have seen us seriously injured, such was the force of the wind. We made for the lee side of a small knoll, and ever so carefully removed the bivvy shelter from its bag, keeping it compressed until a momentary lull in the wind speed enabled us to whip it quickly over the top of us and tuck it under our rucsacs, on which we then sat. These bivvy shelters have no structure, and with no poles to help keep them rigid, they have a tendency to flap and billow in strong winds unless sufficient people sit around the internal circumference to keep things snug. Ours rippled and snapped like a mainsail gone mad and its tension pulled us this way and that as we attempted to wrest some sort of control. A few nips and tucks in the nylon and readjusted rear ends did the trick, and we settled down to examine our casualty in comparative warmth and calm. We confirmed that he was uninjured, but suffering from the first stages of hypothermia and he certainly required evacuation – there was no way he was going to walk off himself.

Hypothermia, or exhaustion-exposure as it is sometimes known, is a relatively common condition on the fells. It manifests itself when the body is unable to maintain its normal temperature, and its heat production becomes increasingly centralised around the body's core. Typically, this is caused when the external tempera-ture is low, in particular when combined with wind and wet, and when the victim's clothing and metabolism is unable to cope. It is further exaggerated if the person involved is tired, has had a poor food intake or is ill. The symptons of hypothermia are varied, but can include feeling cold and tired, lagging behind the main party, erratic or unusual behaviour which can be aggressive, general lethargy and disinterest. As the condition becomes more severe, the body temperature continues to decline, the victim becomes increasingly cold and tired and will eventually lose consciousness and die, unless given appropriate assistance. Young people are especially susceptible to hypothermia, although anyone exposed to low temperatures for long enough will succumb. In British mountain regions, it's the wet and wind rather than just the cold which really cause problems and the importance of good equipment both to repel water and to prevent the next-to-skin layer staying wet cannot be overstated.

In this case, our lost but found walker was wet, exposed to severe winds and low temperatures, and was physically tired. His good clothing and equipment had undoubtedly helped to stave off the worst effects of the night's inclemency, but we had to ensure that he was kept as warm as possible to prevent any further deterioration. We had radioed Ambleside base and informed them of our discovery, along with details of our location. We were also able to communicate with other team members who were searching on the ridge, so we hoped to have company shortly.

Our decision was that we would have to carry our casualty off by stretcher, but the choice of route was not as simple. Our position on the Crinkles was fairly central, giving us the possibilities of descending via Red Tarn and Wrynose Pass, via Three Tarns and the Band, or into Eskdale or Mosedale. Each descent had advantages and problems but, whatever the choice, we could not possibly carry the casualty along the ridge due to the winds. It was at this point that I think we made a fundamental mistake in choosing to descend via Three Tarns and the Band.

The first arrivals to locate us on this wild and windswept ridge were a group of search dog handlers, headed by Malcolm Grindrodd and Dave Riley. Although there is no doubting the skills of the handlers and the abilities of the dogs, it just didn't work here and they got a bit of stick after having to home in on our lights when the dogs failed to find us. Our numbers slowly increased until we both had a stretcher and enough personnel to carry it. The decision concerning the descent route was probably a collective one. I'm not sure. But in retrospect I would have like a second opinion from some of the Eskdale team members regarding descents to that side. The problem was that due to the severity of the wind, we had to contour on the Eskdale side of the Crinkles ridge to gain Three Tarns, and this is a tortuous route which crosses boulderfields, scree, jutting ridges and sodden bogs. Given good daylight visibility we might have been able to choose a better route, but in the conditions we experienced that night, staggering along with the stretcher on the easiest route our scouts could find was the best we could do. About 4.30 am we had to stop. Most of us were very wet, despite good quality gear and fatigue was obvious to see as progress slowed, mistakes increased and tempers frayed.

We squatted down in amongst some boulders which offered seats and a little shelter, slung the group shelters around us and shivered away the rest of the night until a miserable grey dawn and increasing cold stirred us into action again. For me, the rest of the carry to Three Tarns is recalled as a purgatory experience of simple endurance. It's hard work carrying a stretcher in normal conditions, but with that combination of difficult terrain and severe weather it became a desperate struggle and I don't mind saying that it exhausted me. The final descent from Three Tarns was lightened when a new party from the Kendal team arrived and took over the carry, but no matter who was carrying the stretcher, it doesn't alter the fact that the Band makes for a long descent, and it wasn't until about 9 am that we finally reached the farmyard at Stool End. At that point I recognised the first signs of hypothermia in myself, after twelve hours of constant effort in such conditions and with waterproofs which I found had leaked like a sieve, wetting me to the skin. I have been out for much longer periods in much lower temperatures, but never experienced the same fatigue and cold rendered by that typical Lakeland winter's night. We found out later that the winds had been of storm force, gusting to

90 mph. A force 10 gale by comparison is 55–63 mph on the Beaufort Scale.

So how can you avoid becoming another bad weather statistic in the annals of mountain rescue? Firstly, you should not have fixed goals. Too many walkers have their sights set rigidly on a certain peak or route, and attempt it whatever the conditions. Your route for the day should take into account the current and forecast conditions, and that lower level walks can be far more interesting and enjoyable than high level trogs in the wind, rain and hill fog. Secondly, you should always get a forecast before setting out, and preferably use this in conjunction with common sense and personal weather forecasting skills. There are some excellent books on the subject. (Weather forecasting, not common sense I should add!) Next, you should allow enough time to complete your chosen route. One of the most common reasons for walkers becoming overdue and subsequently benighted is that the walk has taken much longer than expected. The use of a simple formula based on the well-known Naismith's Rule (10–12 minutes per kilometre and 1 minute for every 10 metres of ascent) enables accurate calculations to be prepared, and the problem avoided. Your navigational skills should be good – can you identify your position on any mountain to within fifty yards in all conditions, day and night? The right map is also useful. Using those contained in the back of a diary, as more than one person has been seen doing, is not to be recommended! A torch is essential during the winter months, along with a spare battery and bulb, and to ease the predicament of benightment you should carry spare food, clothing and an emergency shelter. Even one of the basic giant plastic bag type can be a lifesaver. The consequences of becoming lost in bad conditions, and subsequent benightment, could be as slight as an uncomfortable night's sleep and a good story to tell, but sadly, for others, the sleep is permanent and the story never told.

4

WINTER IN LAKELAND

Winter in the Lake District is an erratic and unpredictable affair. Our mountains are just too close to the Irish Sea, the winds able to breathe in the warmth from the Gulf Stream and radiate its gentle heat over the fells, producing rapid thaws which sap the spirit as fast as they melt back the snow and ice. If the Lakeland fells were further east, centred around the northern Pennines, we would have longer and harder winters to look forward to, ski areas probably, and even more roads blocked by snow and ice than the current highway authority allows. Maybe it wouldn't be such a good thing after all! I really ought to mention in passing the new gritting policies of Cumbria Highways department in the Langdale area. Following on from self-service petrol and food, we now have self-service gritting. Dumps of road salt are provided in luminous green bins and the motorist invited by suggestion to do the job him- or herself. In some locations, the piles of salt are just dumped on the verge, and become invisible every time it snows. Very helpful.

In a typical Lakeland winter – if there is such a thing – the first dusting of snow on the fells appears somewhere between the end of October and mid-November. This snow rarely lasts, and like a ptarmigan or mountain hare acquiring their ghostly winter coats, gaining a full cover takes time. Major snowfalls often occur between mid-January and April, but it is the early ones which really count, for they provide the base on which further snowfall can accumulate and adhere. Good walking and climbing conditions could occur at any time during the period from November to April, after which the warm spring sunshine usually gets to work on the remaining snow banks, which shrink steadily to disappear finally in June. There are exceptions of course. In 1994 snow fell towards the end of October, and the fells were white for almost three weeks, the only time I have ever skied in the area as early as that.

Recently there has been a trend towards warmer autumns and colder springs, with some exceptionally cold weather in April and even May, when easterly winds have swept bitter conditions across from eastern Europe. The winter of 1995–6 was the hardest for many years, and was also unusual in other ways. The period between the middle and end of December brought exceptionally low temperatures and severe frosts, and it was the first time for fourteen years that many of the low-level waterfalls froze hard enough to climb. The inevitable thaw started on New Year's Day and a short respite gave warmer conditions until the middle of the month, when cold easterlies set in once more. Two weeks of biting winds straight out of Siberia gave us another spell of superb ice climbing conditions, and there wasn't a fellside in the region without smears and streaks of blue ice, where springs, streams and trickles normally flowed. Despite the cold winds, there was almost no snow at all, and at the beginning of February, the valley of Oxendale at the head of Langdale and the knobbly outline of Crinkle Crags above displayed autumnal colours below a vivid blue sky, the only sign of winter being the ragged streaks of blue ice bisecting every ghyll and stream in the area.

Then a couple of days later it snowed – for thirty-six hours. In the heaviest snowfall for at least forty years between two and three feet of snow lay level throughout Langdale, with drifts much deeper. Minor roads were closed for a minimum of two days and I did not manage to get a vehicle out of my drive for three, though this could have had something to do with the fact that building igloos, snowballing and skiing were much more fun than shovelling feet of snow. This snowfall was unusual in its depth, and unusual in that it fell on hard frozen ground which offered little cohesion. The result – conditions in which avalanches were quite likely, though predicting when and where they were most likely to happen was extremely difficult, due to the lack of comparative situations in previous years.

It may surprise some readers to learn of the frequency of avalanches on the Lakeland fells. They are not an unusual or isolated event and, though generally not as dangerous and as large as those affecting the Scottish mountains, they can and do injure and kill both walkers and climbers. There are many different types and classifications of avalanche, and the subject is so complex, it is impossible to do it anything near justice here. However, there are certain factors and conditions in which avalanches are much more likely. After new snowfalls, the danger tends to be most acute. It is generally accepted that up to a foot (30 cm) of new snow gives low-risk, up to two foot medium-risk and up to three foot high-risk conditions.

Avalanches occur when a mass of snow on a slope reaches a point at which it cannot adhere to the surface beneath, and gravity causes it to slide downwards. If the fall is in still conditions, sloughs of new snow are common. These tend to break away from a single point and form a characteristic teardrop shape. Though often relatively small, they can easily be large enough to bury a mountaineer and they can often be seen in the eastern corries of Helvellyn, Nethermost and Dollywaggon, for example. These heavy snowfalls in windless conditions are very rare in this area. More often than not, the snowfall is accompanied by strong winds, conditions which can give rise to deceptively dangerous conditions for the uninitiated. As the wind blasts the snow crystals, it changes their shape, and rounds them off, making them less likely to adhere to the snow surface they fall on. In the lee of the wind, these crystals create slabs of snow which can vary between very soft and hard enough to stand on without sinking. This resultant windslab, as it is known, can feel deceptively secure. In reality, it may break off over a wide distance, and to a depth of several feet if enough snow has been blown over. Particularly worrying is the fact that this sort of avalanche is almost always triggered by the walker or climber themselves, the extra weight which the slab is having to bear being just too much. The avalance does not have to be too big either. Just enough to sweep you from your feet may be sufficient to cause a serious accident. Windslab snow can be recognised by its frequently chalky appearance, its tendency to squeak when walked on, and the way in which small slabby chunks break off beneath one's feet.

Avalanches also occur in thaw conditions, as water runs between different snow layers, or between the snow and the ground, acting as a lubricating layer which can lead to wet snow avalanches. Slower than dry snow, they are nonetheless just as perilous and, once stopped, the resulting debris sets like concrete. Again a major player in the avalanche stakes, the wind, can create cornices, great arches of snow that defy gravity and lean crazily out over voids. These can be dangerous in all conditions. Last year, two walkers took a bearing from the top of Swirral Edge on Helvellyn, to the summit trig point, but did not allow for the sweeping curve of the corrie headwall. As a result, in bad visibility, they both fell straight through the cornice. One of the walkers described to me how one second he was walking comfortably, the next he was in freefall, spinning and spiralling at a great rate down towards Red Tarn. Both managed to stop themselves by applying an ice axe brake. Others are not so skilled and fortunate, though there are many instances of climbers, walkers, dogs, skiers and snowboarders falling the full length of this wall of snow and walking away at the bottom unharmed. As always with slips on snow, it's what you might hit on the way down which is the problem.

Cornices can also become extremely heavy during periods of

thaw, their increasing weight eventually sending them hurtling downwards. I have seen blocks of snow the size of small cars at the foot of the Red Tarn face of Helvellyn after such events. Incidentally, most avalanches occur on slopes of between 30 and 45 degrees, though they can occur between 20 and 60 degrees and have been recorded on slopes as low as 17 degrees.

The complexity of avalanche forecasting is heightened by temperature changes, wind speed and direction and slope angle and shape. If you are interested in the subject, there are many books on avalanches and practical courses in snow stability assessment. Good basic advice would be to avoid steep slopes for at least twenty-four hours after heavy snowfall and to learn how to perform simple shear tests.

These are designed to give some indication of the strength of the weakest layer in the snowpack. First, a block of snow twelve to fourteen inches square and at least three feet deep is isolated from the rest of the snow, usually with the aid of a snow saw or ice axe. A ski or ice axe is inserted to the rear of the free-standing snow column, and pressure progressively applied along the full height of the block. The ease with which the weakest layers shear off gives some indication of the potential risk. The test can also be carried out by cutting away the front and sides of the block, and leaving the rear of it attached to the rest of the snowfield. One member then approaches the block from the snowfield above, and the rest observe the ease with which the block shears, and the exact location of the split. Done frequently, this can give accurate information about the slope's stability and is recommended if you have to cross any slopes of between 30 and 45 degrees. Look, too, at the weather both before and during your visit to assess which slopes may have windslab and look for any signs of recent avalanche activity. If in doubt, take an alternative route.

Back to the winter of 1995–6, and the avalanche danger created by such a heavy single fall. In Langdale, at least two avalanches occurred where I know of none before. The first was on the road to Blea Tarn, where a car was knocked from the road, though fortunately no one was inside at the time. The second was on the banks of Dungeon Ghyll, in as innocuous looking a place as you could wish to find. This one was approximately twenty yards wide and fell a distance of a hundred yards into the ghyll. At the same time, a huge avalanche in Patterdale claimed the life of a walker, when a slab over fifty yards wide slipped several hundred yards down a steep grassy fellside. Avalanches claim many victims in Scotland, but fatal avalanche incidents in the Lake District are relatively rare. There are a number of accident black spots, such as the top of Central Gully on Great End which regularly avalanches, and which has offered an early descent to the pub to some leading mountaineers, including Alan Hinkes, one of our most talented and likeable Himalayan climbers. Avalanches take no notice of reputation.

The eastern corries of the Helvellyn region, which claimed three lives in one incident in 1984, are another danger area. A group of Venture Scouts were trying to climb what in normal conditions is relatively easy ground at the back of Nethermost Cove. In the hard conditions of the day, with fresh snow underfoot, driving winds and blizzards, the climb would have been both arduous and fraught, and to this day one might ponder the eternal question as to why they attempted the route at all. Sadly, they had no climbing gear, no ice axes or crampons and no helmets. The avalanche swept them down the gully and resulted in three young men losing their lives, and three others sustaining serious injuries. Tragedies such as this inevitably bring wildly differing responses, generally pola-rised into those who think that the group should never have left the valley, and those like Tom Fynn of the Patterdale Mountain Rescue Team who was directly involved in retrieving the three dead youths and their injured colleagues: 'If climbers reckon they can handle the conditions and are well-equipped – good luck to them.'

The incident highlights many points about winter hill walking and mountaineering. The need for the correct equipment and training to match is paramount and there is no doubt in my mind that those involved were inadequately equipped for their climb. Yet I could easily turn round and remember similar incidents in which I have been equally badly equipped, especially in the early years of my climbing career, incidents in which luck and the energies of youth played a greater part than skill and judgement in providing a successful outcome. It is easy to criticise, but harder to recall the learning experiences which we all go through, when our sheer enthusiasm for adventure and our over-zealous pursuit of challenges has maybe put us in similarly dangerous positions. That old adage 'There but for the grace of God . . .' is particularly apt in this instance, although those who engage in sweeping condemnation would probably never understand the naked truth of this.

The Helvellyn area is a magnet for walkers and climbers during the winter months. Its great headwall above Red Tarn holds the most reliable snow in the district and its bounding ridges, Swirral and Striding Edge, provide a spectacular horseshoe unmatched in the Lake District. The terrain to the west is gentler and more rounded, providing good access in all conditions, but this eastern side is quite different. Snow may lie here long after it has completely disappeared from the Thirlmere side, the gullies etched as ribbons of white snaking up to a continuous rim of snow which lines the plateau. Whilst conditions in the valley can be delightfully spring-like, winter still holds court at high level and it is icily unforgiving in its treatment of those who pay it little respect. No mountain in the Lake District attracts such numbers of ill-prepared and ill-equipped walkers during the winter months, and no mountain has such a dreadful accident record.

It was half way along the narrow section of Striding Edge that I saw my first mountain accident. We sat astride the rocky crest eating sandwiches and watching a group of climbers making their way steadily up the easiest slopes above Red Tarn. When they reached a point about a rope-length below the final corniced lip, one climber fell, and cartwheeled down the slope like a tiny rag doll, stopping abruptly a hundred feet lower, and remaining worryingly still. We dispatched one member of our group to alert the rescue team, whilst we hurried to the stretcher box, which at that time was positioned at the eastern end of the edge. We carried the stretcher and first aid kit as fast as we dare across the frozen wastes of Red Tarn and ever more slowly up the steepening slopes towards the casualty.

I am certain the others shared my dread at the possibility of being the first people on the scene with any first aid or rescue experience, limited though it was, and we were all visibly relieved when we came across the reassuringly commanding figure of Roy Harding, one of the National Park Rangers, with his huge alsatian, who I think was called Banner. Roy had already called out the rescue team via his radio, and we helped patch up the climber, who had relatively few injuries – a broken arm, ankle and various cuts and bruises. Along with other climbers who had volunteered their services, we loaded him onto the stretcher and carried him off towards the tarn outflow, from which point the rescue team took over.

This sort of self-help, particularly if there were one or two people present with first aid or rescue skills was very effective, and the casualty in this instance was removed from the fells considerably faster than would have been the case if he had waited for the team to arrive and perform the full evacuation themselves. Sadly, this can no longer happen. Vandalism and theft from the rescue boxes led to their removal and a major element of self-help has been lost. Their removal could also have been a blessing for those who might seek alternative shelter during heavy rain, as a man did at the old Rescue Post at Styhead. Seeking refuge from a particularly drenching shower, he climbed into the rescue box. This was fine, except that the door fell shut (accidentally one presumes), and could not be opened from the inside. Some time later, passers-by heard the knocks and shouts and released the man from what could have been an untimely and extremely premature coffin. I can think of fewer greater ironies than dying after accidentally locking oneself in a box intended to provide life-saving equipment!

In the winter of 1994 I took a friend, Nick Owen, who was one of the deputy leaders of the Langdale Team, to try the sport of Upskiing. The near disaster with Gustav Fischnaller had not dampened my missionary zeal. We set out from Greenside mines and took the track to Sticks Pass, which had an Alpine feel to it, with large patches of old snow giving way to fresh green vegetation. Though the snow was thawing at lower levels, above 2000 feet it was rock hard, with an icy crystalline glaze. We enjoyed some fine north-westerlies on Whiteside and Raise and some great skiing in bright sunshine took us across to beneath Helvellyn Low Man.

We decided that we would complete the day by climbing one of the classic easy routes on the Red Tarn face, and after slogging our way up the pleasant ridge to Low Man, we located the top of Swirral Edge and prepared to descend. Conditions were immaculate. Every patch of snow had consolidated to an icy névé, perfect for climbing on, the visibility was excellent and the snow swept in continuous runnels down to the tarn, punctuated only by occasional outcrops of black rock which jutted menacingly from the pristine white slopes. We descended the edge, crampons biting satisfyingly into the hard ice, eyes feasting on the beauty of the feathered slivers of ice which spread out from every rock, and hearts racing with anticipation of the superb climbing conditions. We stopped a while, more to take in the magnificence of the surroundings than the need for a rest, and glanced up at the hoar-rimmed ridge to see a small party descending towards us.

The fall happened so quickly, yet it seemed as though we were watching in slow motion. The cause appeared to be a stumble down a short step in the ridge, but it was the next few seconds which will always live so clearly in my memory. After the fall, her acceleration down the witheringly hard and icy slope was terrifying. Though she tried to effect a brake with her axe, after the first brief seconds it was impossible, such was her velocity, and she sped inevitably downwards, spinning and tumbling, axe flailing wildly, until she eventually came to rest several hundred feet lower after careering over several small outcrops of rock. As the other members of her group came towards us, I recognised Simon, an experienced hill walker who I knew from a course I had been instructing on. The fallen walker was his girlfriend, Rosemary. Urging extreme caution to everyone who descended – the first priority in dealing with an accident is to ensure that no one else gets hurt – we came as near as possible in the conditions to a run down the snow slope, which was so hard that without crampons any progress other than distressingly rapid and downhill would have been impossible.

Rosemary lay huddled on the slope next to a small rock outcrop and, as we neared, I have to admit fearing the worst, for we had seen her bounce over some extremely gnarly terrain which made me wince to watch. I bent down and spoke to her, to get a surprising and reassuringly coherent reply. Despite our protests, she sat up, and miraculously appeared to have sustained no major injuries. Whilst Nick tried to contact Patterdale rescue team on his radio, we and some other climbers who had arrived on the scene cut a ledge in the snow, sat Rosemary on it and enveloped her in the physical and psychological comfort of a small nylon bivvy shelter. We examined her thoroughly, still expecting to find some evidence of more severe injury, but apart from a minor head cut and a possible ankle injury there was nothing to show. Nick had contacted Patterdale, but his radio batteries were fading so, though we knew the message had got through, we had no knowledge of the team's response. It was going to be dark in an hour, and Rosemary was still a few hundred feet above Red Tarn, with some awkward terrain to descend. After half an hour or so, in which time we were able to establish that her condition was stable, we decided that we would have to move her down to the tarn to speed up the evacuation process. While Simon and a couple of other helpful climbers descended and sliced resting ledges from the hard granular snow, Nick and I roped Rosemary up and half lowered, half supported her on her gentle downward progress.

Half an hour of hard effort on her part brought us to a flatter area near the shore of the ice-bound tarn, where we cut a good ledge from the snow and re-enveloped her in the bivvy shelter. We were surprised that no rescuers had arrived – after all, a fast walker would be able to get to Red Tarn in under an hour from Greenside, and it was now at least an hour and a half since we had requested assistance. Another half hour passed, then an hour, by which time we were all cooling down and keen to start moving again. Almost three hours after the alarm was raised, we had a small group of Patterdale rescuers alongside, strangers mostly to us, soon supplemented by support from the Penrith team. All our initial questions to Rosemary were posed again by this new wave of support, and her answers reiterated. First aid was repeated a second time, the situation reassessed, and Nick and I were left wondering if we were perhaps invisible, or maybe smelled particularly badly, as no one seemed to want our opinion. Rosemary was eventually evacuated by helicopter almost four hours after the initial call-out. She made a speedy recovery, suffering only a minor foot injury in what seemed at the time to be an horrendous fall.

The only post-mortem which had to be carried out here was to examine the reaction and organisation of the rescue operation. Several main points sprang out. Nick and I should have had a spare battery to back up the one in the radio. After all, if you're going to carry it, it might as well be usable, and we should have been able to communicate with other rescuers at a later stage, which would have been of benefit to all. The length of time which elapsed before a response from the local team was forthcoming was unacceptably long. In fact the rescue operation would have been faster if we had called out the Langdale team to deal with the incident, despite the fact that they would have had to travel further. I have no idea why the delay was so long, except that the Patterdale team had already been out on at least one other call-out that afternoon. But rather than trying to cope with everything that was happening, I think they should have called for assistance from other teams sooner. It was also noticeable that, despite Nick and I having been with the casualty right from the start, and the fact that both of us were experienced rescuers, some of the local team members were extremely reluctant, almost to the point of rudeness, to involve us once they had arrived. This mirrors the underlying resentment and mistrust that exists between many rescue teams, their unwillingness to involve others and their geographical exclusivity. Though individual members retain strong friendships with those from other teams, the depth of some of the ill-feeling between teams would surprise many onlookers.

The most remarkable winter accident I have ever come across, or indeed ever heard of, occurred on Pavey Ark. South-facing and at relatively low altitude, Pavey has never been a major winter climbing crag, but in hard conditions its main gully lines can be choked with thick ice, and the narrow gash taken by Little Gully is something of a classic. An old picture I saw recently showed the crag in its finest winter garb, with huge white fangs of ice draped over its smooth slabs, and with every groove and crack packed tight with snow. Hoar frost and powdery snow cast a pale grey shimmer over every other inch of its pock-marked rock and the rough screes beneath lay under extensive drifts. If conditions like that ever reappear, Pavey Ark will instantly produce many classic ice and mixed routes in the modern idiom. It's only a pity that they could only ever be climbed so infrequently.

In an average winter however, the Langdale Pikes, of which Pavey Ark forms an integral part, receive precious little snowfall and, despite resembling Alpine or even Himalayan giants immediately after heavy falls of snow, it rarely lingers. The biggest accumulations occur here when a strong north-westerly wind plies the south facing slopes with vast amounts of powdery spindrift, a process which can occur long after the actual snowfall has stopped. The winds gather light loose snow from the vast moorlands behind the imposing Langdale faces of these mountains, and whip it into a spiralling air-driven maelstrom of stinging white. It blows like an eternal duststorm until the snow has nowhere else to go but down into the eddying shelter of gullies, hollows and crags. In this way, huge quantities of snow can accumulate in certain areas in the lee of the wind, and it was in conditions such as this, with Pavey Ark plastered white, that the accident happened.

The mountaineer in question was making an ascent of Jack's Rake, the familiar fault line which rends the cliff from bottom right to top left as if sliced by a mighty knife. The scramble up the Rake is for the most part comfortably enclosed, those ascending it being sheltered from the awesome views down towards Stickle Tarn by its gully-like formation. There are, however, one or two sections which command a little more respect. The most obvious is a flattening in the Rake where the great sweep of Crescent Slabs rises to meet the inverted crescent from which its name originates. Climbers who have ascended the slab must then wander up a steep slope of grass and broken rock to gain the Rake, which at this point is narrow and minus the security of its usual channel. In hard conditions, the pathway along the Rake can be smeared with ice and choked with snow, turning it into an entirely different proposition to the pleasant scrambling found during dry summer weather, sufficient for it to be given a Grade 1 snow climb status.

David Birkett, one of my fellow National Park Rangers, was at Stickle Tarn that day. Looking across the frozen water to the vertical wasteland of Pavey Ark, he saw something which every walker and climber fervently hopes they will never see – a body falling and crashing down the flanks of the cliff. The fall was at least 200 feet, probably a little more, and took place over a mixture of vertiginous, bare rock and icy streaks. When the body came to a halt at the foot of the crag, David was convinced that serious injury or death was a certainty, and he immediately used his radio to call for assistance. After hearing the call-out details on my radio, I met other team members at the New Dungeon Ghyll Hotel, and we set off up towards the tarn. A helicopter had been called in immediately, due to the nature of the incident, and was expected at the tarn shortly after our estimated arrival time. I think Tony Richards and I arrived there first and we expected to be continuing our walk to the screes at the foot of the crag to recover a body.

However, to our utter and no doubt undisguised amazement, David and the casualty were sitting down by the dam. Delighted that he had been able to walk down and that his only injuries appeared to be minor cuts and bruises, we assumed that his fall must have been relatively short. How wrong we were. Over 200 feet up from the foot of the crag, and at the flattening on the Rake previously mentioned, a groove in the snow could be spotted with the naked eye. This was the start of his slide. He must have accelerated down here with the ferocity of a Ferrari, then been launched like Eddie the Eagle over the edge of Cresent Slabs to tumble down rock and ice until he hit the bottom, where, miraculously, his fall had been broken by a deep snowdrift. Alton Towers has nothing like this. As the helicopter lifted him off for a check-up, I traced his line of fall down the grooved snowslope and down the line of what is a Severe rock climb in dry conditions. No matter how I looked at it, I could see no outcome other than severe injury or worse and, to this day, whenever there is snow on Pavey I can still visualise that groove which his slide had carved into the snow. That he was not killed was amazing. That he also walked down to the Tarn was beyond credibility.

Recent years have seen a massive increase in the popularity of winter hill walking and climbing, a trend which has altered visitor patterns to our mountain areas, increasing the pressure on sensitive sites and also produced some excellent new equipment designed to cope with severe conditions. It has also rather unfortunately given the media plenty to whinge about, and several well-publicised rescues in Scotland have given a completely false impression of the dangers of tackling the hills and crags in their winter raiment. Incidents involving avalanches, falls and benightment have been thrust upon the general public by the media in an unprecedented burst of enthusiastic reporting. Winter accidents on the mountains have become a magnet for popular journalism, with results which the vast majority of hill-goers despised.

Firstly, there was the speedy uptake by politicians on the insurance theme. Climbing is dangerous! You must be insured! Rescues cost lots of money! (Plus the hidden agenda of gaining brownie points by appearing to be concerned and responsible individuals, not to mention the money which insurance companies could command and the bureaucracies which could be created.) Supposedly concerned individuals (most of whom I had never heard of before) sprang up from nowhere to preach the insurance gospel and to cast suspicion and doubt about the need for people to go into the hills in winter at all. It's foolhardy, negligent and puts the lives of others at risk they castigated. These people clearly did not listen to the opinions of mountaineers and rescuers. We did not and do not want insurance schemes. We believe that individuals should have the freedom to revel in the challenges and adventure presented by the natural environment. We believe that mountaineering should be as bureaucracy-free as possible, and that restrictions, registering, compulsory certificate-ticking and the like have no place in our sport. Rescuers may sometimes criticise those who push the boat out a little too far in bad conditions, but they are dead against insurance schemes and pledge that their voluntary, though highly professional, work will continue. They may preach safety and urge those venturing out in the harshness of winter to be prepared, well-equipped and trained, but they want restrictions and insurance as much as they want marshmallow ice axes.

An interesting postscript into the media hype was the way in which some individuals cashed in on the huge amounts of publicity given over to their predicaments. Certain individuals received considerable sums of money for telling their stories in the tabloids or for endorsing certain products, and there were rumours that one disappearance and subsequent miraculous discovery after several nights in the snow was pre-planned and intentionally aimed at making a healthy profit. After all, surviving a few nights in a well-prepared snowhole is not that difficult – climbers and skiers in Norway and many other major snow-holding regions live in snowholes for their weekends away or multi-day expeditions. Incidentally, just in case any readers may be marketing executives looking for a good idea, I'd be quite happy to survive a few nights in a snowhole of my choice on certain brands of beer and chocolate in return for a healthy fee!

It is in a snowhole you can best survive a blizzard, though if you've never been in the sort of ferocious storm which can sweep areas such as the Cairngorm Plateau, it will be hard to imagine the malevolence and brutality of the conditions. In a true blizzard the wind can reach strengths exceeding one hundred miles per hour, rendering anything other than a crawl impossible. Grains of snow blown at these speeds penetrate every minuscule gap in clothing and equipment and they can freeze your eyelids tightly shut in seconds. Attempting to read a map or use a compass is useless, and the complete lack of visibility – white out as it is known – makes it impossible to differentiate between slope angles, upsets balance, creates disorientation and generally confuses. Even breathing can be difficult. The low temperatures and terrific wind-chill combine to extract heat from your body more quickly than you can replenish it and, without shelter, extended survival is impossible.

Two serious incidents in the Lake District, thirty-five years apart, illustrate the consequences of becoming caught in blizzard conditions. The first happened on Easter Monday in 1951, when two girls set out at 9.30 to walk from Grasmere to Ambleside. At 10.30, the white swirl of a venomous blizzard struck the area. The girls failed to arrive at their destination and at the time it was considered unthinkable that they might possibly have ventured off the easy tracks and roads which link the two villages. Any suggestion that they might have lost their way on the fells was dismissed, due to the conditions on the day. Numerous searches and appeals were made and several sightings were reported, including that they had been seen dismounting from a bus in Langdale, but they could not be found. A week later, hundreds of volunteers searched the area, rambling clubs, Police, farmers and shepherds joining forces in a common goal, but not a trace of the missing girls was found. Many days later a local man spotted a speck on the upper slopes of Fairfield which turned out to be a piece of clothing. The body of a girl was found beneath the snow, possibly as a result of having fallen through a cornice. Two weeks later, a local doctor's blood-hound stopped and scratched at a bank of snow, so discovering the second body.

The second incident also raised the pay for rescue issue, which has reared its head on a number of occasions. In 1986 there was a call for compulsory insurance by the local newspaper, the *Westmoreland Gazette*. This followed an incident in Kentmere, in which a hundred rescuers searched for two missing groups in foul night-time conditions. Whoever wrote the *Gazette*'s editorial at the time obviously felt that this was completely unjustifiable, and that the threat of having to pay for the rescue would be sufficient to deter mountain-goers from attempting anything other than a stroll up Wansfell on a warm summer's afternoon.

Perhaps now, the time has come for Mountain Rescue Teams to question their own approach to safety on the fells. It is surely not good enough to dismiss an operation involving 100 people as 'bad luck' for those rescued because they were well equipped. Walkers and climbers at times appear not to consider the risk to life and limb, either their own or other people's. But those who put others at risk would surely think twice if they had to make some financial contribution.

I suppose we do have to remember that this was in the middle of the Thatcher years, when everyone had to be answerable to someone, unless, of course, you were Prime Minister, everything had to be charged for and nothing was worth doing unless you got paid for it. Well, were the comments justified?

The initial call-out that day was to the Kendal Mountain Rescue Team, who have the delightful Kentmere valley in their area (though the Langdale/Ambleside team would love to have their area extended to include it). The day had been bitterly cold and dry, though all the weather forecasts were predicting some heavy snowfall later on. By the time the Langdale team were called in to assist, along with those from Patterdale, Penrith, Kirby Stephen and the RAF, conditions had deteriorated significantly, heavy snow was falling and visibility was very poor, even at low level. The only good thing was that the winds were relatively light. We pulled into Hartrigg Farm at Kentmere about 6 pm and made for the reservoir at the head of the valley by Land Rover. In good conditions, this is a beautiful spot and relatively quiet, ringed by the fells which make up the well-known Kentmere Horseshoe.

Some years ago, I was sat overlooking the reservoir whilst the hunt was active on the Ill Bell side of the valley. The hounds set up a huge red deer stag which, though not being chased by the pack, decided that he would do his utmost to avoid detection. He zig-zagged and leapt down the fell in huge jumps, before diving unhesitatingly into the water and swimming across the widest part. For a few brief moments, I thought he might have bitten off too much, but I needn't have worried as, throwing up a visible bow wave to the front, he reached the far shore in no time at all, stumbled out onto the rocky bank and after gancing quickly back towards the hounds, which had long since given up the chase, he bounded up towards Nan Bield Pass looking as fresh as a daisy. I reflected afterwards that perhaps several deer swimming together with a large stag at the front might even look vaguely Loch Ness Monster-like, so you might like to add this to your list of favourite explanations for Nessie sightings.

Loch Ness was certainly not in our minds as we clung onto the roof of our Land Rover as it wobbled and jolted its way in the darkness towards the reservoir, giving us the feeling of being on one of those mechanical rodeo horses in a snowstorm. People were being deployed over some wide areas at the head of the valley, sensibly being asked to keep in small groups and to ensure that everyone kept close together. We were briefed to search an area of very steep ground, mixed scree, rock and grassy banks beneath Thornthwaite Crag. There were about six in our group, and we decided to sweep the area in a series of ever increasing horizontal passes, gaining height each time we came to the ends of our area. This was considerably easier said than done, in no small way due to the difficulty of even locating the correct area for searching. We were equipped with head torches and with a hand-held lamp each, attached to a sling which passed over the shoulder and gave hands-free operation. We had radios, spare equipment and first aid kits and a bivvy shelter, should we have to spend the whole night out, plus Karrimats and either sleeping bags or duvet jackets.

The snow fell even more heavily as we clumped a way towards the base of the steep fellsides. It stuck to our boots (crampons were useless as they would have balled up instantly) and, in deeper accumulations, made us feel as though we were walking through treacle. Despite being aware of the urgency required to find the missing persons, we were unable to proceed as fast as we would have wished. It was like one of those dreams in which you're trying to run faster, and know you can, but your body feels leaden and refuses to respond. Unfortunately, on this occasion we didn't have the luxury of waking up and realising it was all just a bad dream, the nightmare simply continued as reality. For several hours we staggered first one way across the slope, then back again, each time gaining a little height, each time covering a little more important ground. The only interlude in this hard and ceaseless toil was when reports came over the radio that the missing group had been found. We waited with baited breath for the call to return to base, but it never came, for the group which had been discovered was a separate group altogether from the one we were searching for. One of this group had slipped and fallen around 400 feet, sustaining head injuries, bruising and a broken rib. They were airlifted out as conditions improved near to midnight. The search for the original group continued.

We noted that in spite of the copious quantities of new snow, the weather had become much warmer and the fresh wind had died, making the going a little gentler. By 2 am, we had covered our area and found nothing, and even if we didn't care to admit it, we were all extremely fatigued and ready for a rest. We were to be replaced with a fresh RAF team, so made our way back down through the eerie mist to the waiting Land Rover (for a seat inside this time), and a ride back to Hartrigg Farm where a kitchen table (a real farmhouse-sized one at that) full of cakes and sandwiches awaited us. We had eaten little since lunch time, and I suspect the farmers' wives who had risen to the occasion magnificently were somewhat startled to see the rapidity with which their baking was devoured, a bit like pig-feeding time one was heard to remark. Our work done, we headed wearily homewards, the roads now free of snow and the weather clearing.

The next morning we heard that the missing group had been found near Gavel Crag, which was close to where we had been searching at 4 am. One member had hypothermia, one had suffered a broken leg and arm and the other an arm and head injury. They had no winter equipment, and it appeared that in the appalling conditions of late afternoon, they had taken the wrong route off the ridge, wandered onto steep ground and suffered the almost inevitable consequences. They were perhaps fortunate that the snowfall brought higher temperatures with it, otherwise their general condition could have been much worse.

After the event, there were the predictable calls from the local press for charges to be levied on those requiring rescue, in the hope that this measure would dissuade them from taking risks in similar circumstances. There were also calls for rescue teams to adopt a less sympathetic attitude towards the casualties they rescue. But as the leader of the Kendal rescue team, Steve Barber, said at the time, 'When they set out, the weather was reasonable and the snow only came on later.'

No doubt everyone had a view at the time, but I think both of these publicised views are wrong. Charging for rescue is impractical and unpopular, most of all within the rescue teams themselves. It would be nigh impossible to manage and would not have the effect which the *Gazette*'s editorial feature wanted – that of putting people off mountaineering in bad conditions, which in any case are not always possible to predict reliably. Equally, it is only reasonable to expect mountain-goers to take all reasonable precautions against whatever nature may throw at them, including being adequately equipped and skilled, and checking a weather forecast before they set off. This group were reasonably equipped, but had no ice axes or crampons, and they let themselves down in two other ways. Firstly, they failed to take into account the dramatic change in the weather which had not only been forecasted quite clearly, but which was easily predictable at the time by anyone with basic practical weather skills. (The approaching weather front, and its succession of cloud changes were text book in appearance.) Secondly, they did not have the navigational skills to enable them to routefind accurately, skills which are absolutely essential for anyone venturing out in winter conditions. The cause of the accident could therefore be placed squarely at their own feet. They lacked the skills and common sense required for safe winter walking and could blame no one but themselves for the end result. In my view, incidents such as this stress the need for skills training and self-reliance, not for insurance scams – sorry, schemes – and pay-for-rescue ideas.

If you haven't been initiated into the mysterious joys of winter mountaineering, you may wonder what the great attraction is, and why this branch of the sport is currently increasing in popularity at such a rate. I could try to tell you, but I fear any number of words would be sadly inadequate. Instead, I'll just suggest you go and find out for yourself. If you've had plenty of summer hill walking experience, book yourself on a winter skills course and learn the basics, *then* get out and discover!

5

CRAGFAST

The outline of the Langdale Pikes must be the best known mountain outline in Britain. It forms a letterhead or advertising symbol of some sort for dozens of businesses, it graces postcards by the thousand and it presents a magnificent silhouette, visible even from many miles down the M6, that has stirred the hearts of millions. Particularly startling is the huge sweep of rocky fellside which descends, Alpine-like in steepness, towards Mickleden from the summit of Pike O'Stickle, the left-hand summit of the Pikes and the most fascinating. Known as the Sugar Loaf by the local farmers, its summit forms a final rocky nipple atop the sweeping cleavage of Mickleden and the undulating barren wastes of Maiden Moor.

Its fine top is attained by the vast majority of walkers from the soft side to the north, via a short stony scramble which looks much more than it is. To the east, a huge gully plunges down to the scree slopes above the flat valley base. Used for dozens of years as a descent from the summit and also due to the interest provided by Stone Age caves on its side, the gully has become dangerous and unpleasant. Like so many other screes in the area, it is simply worn out. Bare slabs of rock lie like snares beneath a fine camouflage of scree, and loose dusty blocks of dense rhyolite trundle freely downwards, whereas once their descent would have been absorbed and checked by the fine screes. An old National Trust sign warns of the danger, but anyone with twenty-six grams of common sense would realise the problems and take another route.

Round to the west of the summit crags is another gully, less well-known, narrower and sheltered by its own hunched retaining ridge. An exciting winter scramble with a short pitch near the top in hard conditions, it also houses one of the last secret crags in the area. Rather than give too much away, I'll just say that if the crag was conveniently located nearer the valley, say in the position of Raven Crag above the Old Dungeon Ghyll, it would have been stripped of its mossy top coat, brushed and scrubbed, examined with a surgeon's eye for detail and climbed upon by thousands. Don't believe me? You'll just have to go and take a look for yourself! It is the area between these two gullies, overlooking Mickleden, which gives the mountain both its character and its interest.

At valley level, bracken-clad slopes sweep upwards to merge with scree which is frequently punctuated with minor buttresses. Small trees still survive, despite the ravages of the weather and of the local Herdwicks, and the angle slowly steepens until the first rock barrier bars the way to all but the skilled. Above here a series of rock bands separated by grassy ledges leads to a final 160-foot high cone of immaculate rhyolite. Impressive, even awesome from afar, only upon closer inspection does it reveal its true secrets, for it was here that an army of Stone Age workmen quarried axes and other sharp implements which were used over a vast area. A band of hard, flint-like rock provided the raw material and even now, slim flushes of fine scree give away the worksites of centuries ago. It is possible to find rough-outs, part-finished or cast-out axes, but it should be stressed that any disturbance to these ancient sites is completely unacceptable, and I would urge anyone interested to look, but not to touch. Interestingly, a friend of mine from Little Langdale found an axe head on Loughrigg

Terrace – imagine the number of walkers who have walked past, and on, that one!

At the time when these axes were being quarried, the valleys would have been predominantly swampland and the fellsides forested up to around 2000 feet. In the warmer climate of that age, the workers may have lived at high level during the summer months and some evidence of ancient hut circles has been found nearby. Particularly fascinating is the fact that, if you stood on top of Pike O'Stickle and were able to look down into Mickleden in Stone Age times, you would see a populated area with probably more inhabitants than the whole of Langdale has today.

The next major summit of the skyline is the highest of the group, Harrison Stickle. Like Pike O'Stickle, it displays its boldest and grandest profile to the south, though craggy ground falls away from the summit on all sides except those to the north and north-west which yield easy walker's routes. Steep and impressive though it looks, its buttresses are disappointing for the climber, on close inspection being neither sufficiently steep nor continuous to merit more than a passing mention in the climbing guide to the valley. For scramblers though, it ranks with the best – but only for those possessing adequate experience and judgement. Scrambling has become popular. There are several guidebooks extolling its virtues and offering dozens of route suggestions. What many people do not realise is that scrambling is often every bit as dangerous, if not more so, than climbing. On the rocks of Harrison Stickle, for example, the terrain is steep enough for a fall to have dire consequences, the holds are often slippery with moisture, lichen or moss, and loose rock is a continual danger. As most scrambling is done unroped, there is the very real danger that, inexorably, the scrambler will move into an area in which the overall situation demands the same levels of respect, equipment and skills as more serious rock climbing. Adventurous scrambling such as this may offer an admirably pure approach by climbing's ethical standards, but those who stumble face the possibility of paying the ultimate price. The rocks of Harrison Stickle have claimed lives more than once.

Under the western flanks of the peak lies a deep ragged gash, the upper section of Dungeon Ghyll,. This dark cleft houses many Alpine plants, and is judged to be of sufficient botanical interest to be designated a Site of Special Scientific Interest. Budding botanists beware, it is as loose and dangerous as any site of its type and an ascent can only be recommended in hard conditions when, as on major Alpine faces such as the Eiger, the loose material is firmly bonded by the snow and ice.

An incident I recall from the early 1990s involved a call-out into the upper reaches of the ghyll. Once the relevant information had been broadcast, (that stonefall had been heard followed by shouts for help), the first group of rescuers arrived at the New Dungeon Ghyll Hotel and began the gruelling ascent to the plateau beneath Harrison Stickle, from where the approach into the ghyll begins. In order to cover every eventuality, and in particular to ensure that the information we had been given was accurate and that the casualty was not in fact lower down, I made a complete ascent of the gorge from the bottom, whilst genial Jonathan Smith, otherwise known as Hobby Bobby due to his exta-curricular Police duties, peered down into it from its bounding ridge. I recall feeling that this method of ascent was far preferable to the trudge up one of the eroded paths, and it seemed no time at all until we were heading into the upper reaches of the ghyll.

We found the accident site all too easily, at the foot of one of the upper pitches which takes a miserable-looking gully line, edged with precariously balanced boulders. Two climbers lay at its foot, along with evidence of recent rockfall. It appeared that stonefall from above had knocked the lead climber down the gully and also accounted for injuries to the second man. The lead climber's helmet was severely damaged and it was clear that he had head injuries, along with severe lacerations to his hand and a broken ankle. His partner was also wearing a helmet and suffered from a combination of head and other minor injuries. My first thought was that, had they not been wearing helmets, we would have been evacuating at least one body. The lead climber's hat had suffered severe damage and the injuries he might have sustained otherwise really did not bear thinking about.

At this early stage, there were several things to organise. Firstly, we decided that a helicopter was essential, partly in view of the fact that there were two casualties, but also as at least one of the climbers had what appeared to be bad head injuries. This presented a secondary problem in that radio communication from the innards of the gorge were inadequate and necessitated the positioning of a relay on more open ground lower down, through which messages to Ambleside base could be passed. We had to ensure that the correct amount of gear came up from the valley, and that we could find a suitable evacuation route down the ghyll to a site from which the helicopter could evacuate the injured climbers safely.

We also had to monitor the consciousness levels of the two climbers continuously in order to give the hospital the most accurate analysis of their condition during the first couple of hours after the accident. This is of particular importance where head injuries are concerned, as trends in levels of consciousness can give important clues to the medical staff.

We were extremely concerned about the possibilities of further rockfall from above, as walkers finished their day by traversing the path above the ghyll on the flanks of Harrison Stickle. Those in the most exposed positions secured as much shelter as possible from the immediate surroundings, but I think everyone must have felt very vulnerable.

It took some time to get all the gear to site, mainly due to the awkward scrambling involved, but also as there were two casualties. We required two stretchers, ropes and basic climbing gear, first aid equipment, extra helmets and such like. The stretchers in particular can be real awkward pigs to carry. The type in use at the time was the standard Bell stretcher, manufactured locally by team member Peter Bell. Strong and rugged, they have been the most commonly used stretcher in mountain rescue for many years. For carrying, the stretcher splits into two parts, each of which is mounted onto a pack frame, and as long as both rescuers carrying the stretcher end up at the same place it works fine. Though not that heavy, each section's size and shape make carrying quite difficult, particularly in windy conditions, where it feels as though you have a windsurfer sail strapped to your back. Their bulk makes scrambling unpleasant and they will always catch on rocks and branches at the most inconvenient times. On this occasion, scrambling into Dungeon Ghyll was no exception for those involved.

By the time the stretchers arrived, we had equipped the short rock steps in the gorge with ropes so that the casualties could be lowered and protected to back up our manhandling, and a suitable site had been located for the helicopter to winch them aboard. We had carried out as much first aid as was possible without complete mummification and, heartened by the seemingly stable condition of both climbers, we loaded them onto the stretchers and proceeded to evacuate them one by one. The subsequent carry down the ghyll was the epitome of genuine and efficient team work. A main team carried along the easier sections, whilst others descended in front and formed a human conveyor belt to ease the stretcher down the steeper rock steps. Experienced climbers manned the ropes and arranged the fastenings and lowering at lightning speed, though with great security. Having deposited the first casualty at the winching site, we returned for the second and repeated the whole thirty-minute process with equal success. The helicopter arrived on cue, the winching went without a hitch and we suddenly found ourselves alone on the silent fellside accompanied only by the strong feeling of anticlimax which seems to dominate the minutes after the helicopter departs.

We later found out that both climbers made full recoveries – no doubt due in part to the fact that they were wearing helmets – a very satisfying outcome. If anyone were to ask me why I did rescue work, this incident would symbolise my response. A wide variety of team members worked in harmony with each other and a helicopter crew to bring about the successful rescue of two badly injured climbers who lay in an inaccessible and dangerous position, and though it's a great feeling when one's personal skills are called into play in a major way, it's much more satisfying to see a team effort in which everything runs smoothly and in which everyone knows their job and carries it out effectively – particularly when you can look back and know that everything possible was done and that the outcome was successful. 'Everyone's got to know their job and everyone's got to do it properly, otherwise it just ain't gonna work!' This quote from Mission Control, Houston, sums it up well.

The opposite side of Harrison Stickle from Dungeon Ghyll falls away increasingly gently towards Stickle Tarn – the main honeypot of the Langdale fells. Originally two small tarns, a dam was built to flood this spectacular hollow in order to provide a year round water supply for the gunpowder works in Chapel Stile, which lay on the site of the current Timeshare. The dam itself has undergone some major repair work in the last fifteen years and was the scene of one of our greatest public participation experiments, when members of the Ranger Service were asked to take several tons of sand and cement up to the outflow. Not having a helicopter to hand, and somewhat daunted by the thought of having to carry it up ourselves, we set about the task in a completely different way, by dividing the materials into 10–20-pound loads which were placed in poly bags. A large blackboard proclaimed our request: 'Help the National Park repair Stickle Tarn dam – carry a bag up!' The huge pile of bags diminished at a rate appropriate with the path's billing as the busiest in the Lakes, TV and newspaper reporters came to have a look (and went without helping), and in no time at all the job was complete and we were able to press ahead with the repairs. Working on the dam made a good day out, marred only by having to push the occasional wheelbarrow up. Walking up and down, talking to visitors and attempting to extract some of the tarn's lively trout made a hefty dint into the day's work and progress was only maintained thanks to a redoubtable character called Bruce who made the rest of us feel pretty feeble by pushing a wheelbarrow with a full bag of cement in it right up to the dam. The next time you're there, just imagine trying to push 130 pounds in front of you.

These southern flanks of the Langdale Pikes form one of the steepest and most dramatic sweeps of mountainside in Britain, and it is from here, rather than the gentler northern side that most walkers choose to start their ascents. Steep ravines such as Dungeon Ghyll cleave the steepest terrain and broad breasts of land thrust dozens of crags and scree slopes into prominence. The landscape is complex, yet many paths pierce the fellside's rocky armour, taking advantage of the profusion of naturally interconnecting weaknesses and faults.

The precipitous nature of the ground poses many potential pitfalls for the unwary – eroded paths, unstable scree and smooth grass slopes which when wet can possess some similar properties to ice. Alongside these dangers, taking the wrong path, for whatever the reason, can lead to increasingly steep terrain and the possibility of becoming what is locally known as cragfast. Becoming cragfast is not to be recommended. It has only happened to me once in over twenty years of climbing and I would not wish the experience to be repeated. I had only recently started climbing, and the loose-knit group I tagged along with had decided to visit Glencoe for a weekend. It rained as it only knows how in Scotland and conventional climbing was completely out of the question. My climbing partner, Rick Chapman, suggested that we scrambled up a huge gully line which split the roadward side of Buchaille Etive Mor. So armed with a rope and a few slings, waterproofs and a youthful spirit, we squelched across the bogs to regain the foot of the gully.

Its lower section was quite delightful, considering the conditions, consisting of pink waterworn slabs up which we scampered with glee. A few short steeper sections barred the way, but provided no serious obstacle to our frenzied assault. Our determination became somewhat stilted though, at the appearance of the first main waterfall pitch, which formed a steep amphitheatre of vegetated rock, spouting a noisy torrent through its centre which plunged into an evil-looking black pool. The only natural weakness appeared to be up to the right, past clumps of rushes and other lush vegetation, and I elected to lead. After tying our bright orange rope around my waist, adjusting the bowline to a snug fit and remembering to lock it off with a double fisherman's, I set off, cautiously at first, as the rock felt slimy and some holds were of the 'disposable' type. I edged, nudged and squirmed rather than climbed, and came to a point at which a decision had to be made. Above was a small ledge, with a promising piton winking at me from a narrow crack. Once committed on these few moves, retreat looked difficult, but the security offered by the piton provided a tempting bait, as I was already about forty feet off the ground with no protection. I was well and truly hooked, and after shouting my intentions down to Rick, I made the awkward mantelshelf moves to gain a ledge which was narrower than it appeared and also alarmingly loose. Breathing hard, I forced myself to relax. The peg. It was right in front of me and offered so much promise – a can of Boddington's Draught in the middle of a desert. I unclipped a karabiner and snapped it into the comforting eye of the piton, which pulled straight out as soon as I touched it – the can was empty!

Alerting Rick to the problem with a stream of expletives directed at the offending piece of ironmongery, I pondered the situation. Ahead, the rock steepened and appeared more compact. There was no sign of any means of protection and I decided that to continue would have been unjustifiable. That left descending as the only other option, but trying to reverse the awkward mantelshelf move from the loose ledge provided an equally unappealing choice. As the wind and cold rain slowly numbed my fingers, I realised I was stuck. I dare not move up or down, and with great reluctance I had to admit this to Rick.

Our conversation was stilted and wind-whipped, but the

decision was made. He would leave the gully and try to re-enter it higher up and drop a rope to me. Clinging on with one hand, I can clearly recall fumbling with the bowline knot with my other until it came free, after which I watched the rope snake down to Rick, nestling itself in a pool before he hurriedly coiled it. Though it was useless to me, letting it go was traumatic, almost devastating, as it provided such a powerful link between the two of us, even if it were only psychological.

As Rick searched for a route into the gully above me, I waited as calmly as I could, which wasn't really very calmly at all. I was desperately frightened, concerned that the ledge upon which I stood would disintegrate and that the cold and fatigue would get to me before the rope. Ages seemed to pass before I heard from Rick again, but when I did it was with a sense of enormous relief, edged with a tingling excitement in anticipation of what was to come. A few moments later, the rope appeared, thrown too far right. I shouted. Too far right again. I shouted with more venom. Then, like a dart thudding into treble twenty, he got it just right, and the rope slid straight into my outstretched hand. Now it is possible to tie a bowline one-handed, but I couldn't, so my eventual knot was not one which would be found in any textbook on knots or climbing, but it wasn't going to come undone! With a huge cry of 'Climbing!' I set off upwards onto the rock which held so much fear. Now, safely tied to a rope from above, I climbed on auto-pilot, content to use every bad technique in the book in the pursuit of safety. Rick was about a hundred feet higher, but it didn't take long to reach him, and as we stood there, buffeted by wind and rain, I paid my debt of thanks to him right from my heart.

The gully had one final trick up its sleeve however, and as we descended the wind pummelled us from all directions. We gripped the heather and rock as tight as vices, and we had to stop and smother ourselves against the steep hillside as one gust, mightier by far that the rest, swept into the gully with the force of an explosive blast and almost took us with it. After that, the wind calmed to a series of small flurries, like a boxer who had packed everything into one final knockout attempt, failed, and now paced the ring without power or threat. This incident felt like the final, desperate clawing attempt of the mountain environment to destroy us, after which it simply gave up the fight and let us return to safety.

This escapade has left me with at least some recollection of what it feels like to be stuck in a precarious position and, with it, a little understanding of the feelings and thoughts which must have buzzed in the minds of those we have rescued in similar situations. Pavey Ark was again the location for one such incident. The top of Pavey Ark is complex and criss-crossed with sheep trods, the tiny paths which weave in and out of the bilberry and heather and scratch across slabs of knobbly rock. Very tempting these trods, and though for the initiated, they often provide fine traversing routes across difficult terrain, they can also be very misleading, as is the case on Pavey, where many of them terminate in ever steepening rock and then mingle with the vague paths worn by climbers ascending from the more popular routes. For the unwary, they can lead to some serious terrain, though I ought to add that to mistake a trod of this type for the main path off the mountain is like climbing onto a push bike when you are intending to get onto a train.

Maybe it was the occasional bootprint amongst the hoofmarks which caused the confusion, but whatever the reason, the gentleman cragfast on this occasion followed a tenuous track ever downwards, on ever craggier and vertiginous terrain, until he reached some small turfy ledges overlooking the first pitch of a climb known as Rectangular Slab. Beneath him, eighty or ninety feet onto the rift of Jack's Rake, and below that, another 150 feet to the steep grey screes which run down to Stickle Tarn. How he actually reached that point without either realising that he was off route, or without slipping to his death is a mystery which perhaps demonstrates the extraordinary personal qualities which danger and sheer terror can extract from an average person. However, stuck he was, and when the call-out came, we had about two hours before the onset of darkness.

Having the unusual presence of mind to slip a pair of rock boots into my rucsac before departure, I joined a small group in the usual rush up to Stickle Tarn. From car park to tarn would take the average walker between fifty minutes and an hour. In the manic rush of a rescue operation, the walking is considerably faster than this and the ascent is usually made in around twenty-five minutes, though I think Martin Scrowston claimed the fastest time of nineteen minutes. Whatever the time, the result was always the same for me – a feeling of sheer exhaustion and enormous relief that we had reached the tarn and a few minutes of flat walking before the gruelling scramble up the screes to the foot of Jack's Rake. The race to the rescue incident scene was always choked with hidden competition and rife with personal undercurrents. Quite often people only arrived on scene so quickly due to the fear of being overtaken by other team members who were perceived as being older or less fit. It surprised many of the younger team members just how fast the veterans such as Jim Fuller, Iain Williamson or Paul Allonby could be, and a few egos got dented on every call-out. Sarah Hollis was another example. Under five feet tall, she walked like an overwound clockwork soldier and was frequently right up there with the fastest, much to the chagrin of some of the more openly sexist members of the team.

Sexism in mountain rescue? It is not that many years ago that a special meeting was called to discuss whether or not the Langdale team would accept Joy Grindrodd as a member, the daughter of the team's deputy leader! The fact that Joy could outwalk fifty per cent of the existing members did not seem to be relevant – some folk were more concerned with the fact that bawdy jokes and irreverent behaviour might become inappropriate, or that there could be some embarrassment if someone wanted to relieve themselves during the course of the rescue! There were quite a few team members who simply did not want women to join in any circumstances, an attitude which was offensive, negative and backwards-looking, in particular in that the team already had an exemplary and long-serving member in Maureen Richards. Fortunately, this attitude softened, and the increasing number of women in rescue work has demonstrated their value more than adequately to the doubters.

Arriving at the foot of Jack's Rake, I had seen our cragfast walker quite clearly and a small group made their way a short distance up the Rake to the foot of the first pitch of Rectangular Slab. I knew that I could reach him from here after about eighty feet of climbing, but the pitch was graded Very Severe and demanded a little respect. We had about an hour to nightfall, and a speedy evacuation was essential as an operation of this sort would be many times more complex after dark. As we prepared to climb, messages were passed down to ensure all the searchlights were on their way up and that the 300-foot ropes were also prepared for use. Forethought is essential in these situations, and we had to think well beyond what we anticipated as the ideal rescue, into scenarios which involved lengthy abseils from the top of the cliff in the darkness and complex lowers with only the searchlights to provide illumination. Though we still had time to accomplish things in the light, if things didn't go according to plan, we would need all that extra personnel and equipment.

Meanwhile, at the foot of the climb, I slipped on my rock boots and went through the ritual of lacing them tightly, right down to the toes for maximum performance and feel. I took a selection of belaying equipment, a spare harness and rope and set off up the steep rock, which I was relieved to see offered the huge handholds which I remembered from a previous ascent. I placed a couple of nuts for protection on the way and quickly finished the difficult section, heading up and across towards a lonely and frightened figure who sat as still as a piece of porcelain on a mantelpiece. Things looked good. He was on a reasonable-sized ledge with a crack system some way above which offered good anchor points. I made a few reassuring comments whilst assessing the overall situation, and asked him to remain calm and still, and to let me do all the work.

The priority was to make him safe, with the evacuation taking second place at that time. There were a couple of superb nut placements about twenty feet above him, and I linked these together to equalise the pull, clipped a spare rope to them and very steadily abseiled down just to one side of him. One has to assume that, unlike sheep, stranded humans are unlikely to leap from their precarious positions, but one can never be too sure – maybe there were other reasons than simply getting lost for him to be here at all. I also recall an incident in the Dolomites when, on a typically steep limestone wall, about 500 feet from the ground, my wife discovered she suffered from vertigo and for a few moments was determined to jump off. In the end I had to fasten her harness and the rope so she could not undo them!

Taking no chances, I locked off my abseil device and gently crept sideways onto his ledge, keeping on the outside of him all the time to shelter him from the void. I needn't have worried. He didn't want to go anywhere and was clearly, and understandably, very unhappy about his predicament. I slipped a sling around his waist and clipped him to me so that he could not fall, even had he wanted to, and then fastened a harness to him whilst I explained what was going to happen. The blood drained from his face and his voice wobbled as he realised what was in store. 'Have you abseiled before?' was my casual enquiry. The answer was a predictable negative monosyllable. I explained to him that with the onset of darkness so close, the only expedient course of action was for him to have a crash course in abseiling, and to be lowered to the ground with me in control of his descent. This procedure would work perfectly as long as he would relax sufficiently to enable the lower to take place. I explained the situation to him as fully as possible, and demonstrated the techniques we would be using in an attempt to ease his worries, a process which was quite difficult bearing in mind the time constraints we were under. To his eternal credit, he entered into the spirit of things without hesitation and after I had secured the rope to him, and linked it back to the main anchors via a belaying device, he cautiously leant back, committed himself, and began his descent. I lowered him smoothly and steadily into the waiting arms of the rescuers below, where he was unclipped and bustled down the remainder of the Rake just before darkness.

All that remained was a simple abseil down for me and a couple of pints at the Stickle Barn. It is unusual to be in a position to have such an influence on a rescue operation as an individual – they are normally much more team-orientated, but a climbing situation such as this provides one of the very few instances where this is possible. In fact, the rescue had been performed before many team members had even arrived on the scene. If only things always went that well!

Another gentleman who experienced similar problems was Ralph, a Liverpudlian who, like many other Liverpudlians had never set foot on a mountain before, unlike the man in the previous incident who was quite experienced. The incidents did have one major similarity, in that both men inadvertently followed sheep trods lower and lower, down ever steepening terrain until they became utterly stuck. Ralph had been walking on the fellsides above Blea Tarn, a magnificent and popular beauty spot on the pass between the heads of the two Langdales – 'La'al and Big', as they are locally known – and, in a misguided attempt to descend, probably tried to take a direct line to the car park which he would have been able to see. So he had wandered down the heathery slopes above the huge bulk of Blake Rigg, a dark and dank spot on the flanks of Pike O'Blisco, which broods solemnly above the tarn, and landed on his airy perch.

Had this crag been a little higher, a little nearer the road or a little less damp, it would be a popular climbing crag, but these factors have meant that, although routes have been recorded, they have never attained popularity. The crag also hosts a pair of breeding falcons and a wide selection of mountain flora, and climbers and conservationists have enjoyed a satisfactory truce here for years. Though I have visited the crag on many occasions, only one stands out in my memory. We had been searching for falcons as part of a National Park survey, and had gained a ledge system near the crag centre via some awkward climbing. Embarrassingly, we didn't fancy reversing the climb, and continuing upwards was out of the question. We had a short length of rope but no other climbing gear at all to set up an anchor for an abseil or to safeguard any attempt at down climbing.

My companion was Wilf Williamson, and it was he who came up with the bright idea of turning the clock back, and using pebbles jammed into cracks as anchors. 'If Joe Brown and Don Whillans used to do it, it's good enough for us,' said Wilf confidently. Having recently read Don Whillans' book in which he described how some jammed stones almost pulled out of a crack and deposited him and his partner several hundred feet lower, I remained to be convinced. However, we enthusiastically gathered together an assortment of stones from the ledge and proceeded to jam them as best we could in all the cracks we could find. After marking them all out of ten, we picked the best two (which merited scores of four or five each), and tossed a coin to see who would go first. Suffice to say that this was probably the slowest and most gently performed abseil in the history of climbing, but it worked.

Ralph's position was almost directly above this point, about 150 feet higher. He was on the very edge of the steepest part of the cliff and it was difficult to see how he could possibly have landed in such an inhospitable and delicately poised situation.

Gaining access to a cragfast walker or climber is often awkward. Descending from above is generally the safest and easiest method, but great care has to be taken not to exacerbate the situation by accidentally dislodging rocks or dropping equipment. This is a very serious consideration, as many crags which are not popular climbing grounds, such as Blake Rigg, have copious quantities of loose rock, varying from tiny slivers to half-ton boulders, and the vast majority of cragfast individuals have quite enough to contemplate without the need to dodge an arsenal of rocky flak. The alternative approach is from below. This may provide a speedier method of reaching the casualty and making them secure, but it carries a heavier risk for the rescuers. In practice, a combination of the two approaches is often used, especially if skilled climbers are available to make the ascent from below, whilst the others walk round to a convenient abseil location and prepare the ropes for evacuation.

Blake Rigg is a complex crag, continuous and chunky in its centre, but with broken sidewalls of deceptive height which gradually diminish and merge with the steep fellsides. It sports a profusion of bilberry and heather, and in all but the driest conditions remains damp and cool. As we approached the steep slopes beneath the main buttress, we weighed up the situation. Others had already left for the top of the crag, but this was a long approach and potentially time-consuming, as access to the best abseil points is barred by a series of short bands of steep rock. We spotted a possible line of access to Ralph, which involved a rising traverse across a sequence of vegetated corners and slabs, some of which wept slime from grimy cracks. It didn't look hard, but the damp could make it awkward. I was duly elected to go first, a situation I admit to actively encouraging as I love the thrill of lead climbing and in any case would do anything to avoid the long walk to the top of the crag. Grasping clumps of heather and kicking my boots into tongues of rich turf which clung perilously to the slabs, I crabbed across the first twenty feet inelegantly and a little nervously.

The first main barrier was a greasy slab, only ten feet or so across, but devoid of any obvious holds and with only an undercut crack at its top offering any promise of protection. I stretched high and slid my fingers up into the wet slot, pulling out and twisting them at the same time to achieve maximum purchase. Whilst one foot rested comfortingly on the turf, the other crept further and further out onto the slab, until my toe nestled on a tiny edge no more than a few millimetres across. Keeping absolutely still, I reached down to my harness and unclipped a Friend. For the uninitiated, these are aptly named devices which have four expanding cams. Once inserted into a crack, the cams spring out against the sides and hold it in place. Any downwards pull on the device forces the cams ever harder against the crack sides and in theory it grips. In practice it often grips and sometimes doesn't! This particular Friend plunged comfortingly into the crack and, not being able to see its exact position, I just hoped it was well and truly plugged. The move across the slab required finesse, so I was at an immediate disadvantage, but spurred on by the protection offered by the Friend, and by the 'Get on with it' comments drifting up from below, I changed feet on the tiny edge and bridged out onto the far side of the slab to grab yet more fine clumps of heather. A quick swing across and it was all over. Ralph was now comfortingly close with only some easy scrambling left between us.

'Now then Ralph,' I ventured, 'just keep still and we'll have you safe in no time at all.' A few seconds later I stood next to him, at the foot of a blunt rib of dirty rock, and on a ledge big enough to stand comfortably, though a quick rendition of the Hornpipe would have been a non-starter. Whilst quietly explaining to Ralph what was going to happen, I peered about us for some anchor points. If there were any, they were playing hard to get! A tiny spike of rock offered a placement for a thin sling and after some excavation and fiddling, I managed to get a nut jammed half way into a flared crack. I slid a harness around Ralph and clipped him in, reassuring him that help from above would be with us shortly.

The next task involved getting Martin across the traverse and onto the same ledge. He was one of the few team members I would have trusted to climb the pitch in such potentially dangerous conditions, with poor anchors and inadequate protection for a traverse. A slip at any point could have resulted in a pendulum-type fall, and there was no absolute guarantee that I could have held him if the fall was a bad one. As usual, he climbed competently and safely and soon stood next to Ralph and me on the ledge, though I think the smile waned a little once he had seen the anchor points.

Meanwhile, above us, other team members were rigging the ropes ready for an evacuation. Though we had made ourselves as safe as possible on the turfy extrudence which masqueraded as a ledge, we desperately required a rope from above to anchor to for genuine security. We made our request by radio and a few minutes later a rope came snaking down. After making absolutely certain that it was attached to something secure above, we tied Ralph to it, clipped ourselves on with slings and breathed a sigh of relief. It was decided that it would be easier to hoist Ralph up than to lower him to the ground, such was the distance between the anchor points and the foot of the crag, and such was his limited experience of dangling over terrifying drops. We liaised with those above via our crackling handsets and the moment of truth for Ralph finally arrived. But we didn't let him go without giving him a bit of a scare first though. A twisted length of heather root which lay on the edge of the grass bore more than a striking resemblance to a young viper. With my back to Ralph, I carefully leant over and gently picked up the mock snake, before swivelling round, thrusting my hands out in front of him with the stick held out as if it were a dangerous serpent. 'Hey Ralph, a snake!' we shouted. Poor Ralph, in that millisecond it took for him to recognise the stick for what it really was, almost jumped out of his skin. To his credit, he took it well, and afterwards, the situation became so laid back that I doubt he felt any fear at all.

Unfortunately, Ralph's retribution was not yet complete. Hoisting is a rather numb business. It is difficult to assess the force required, and too much rather than too little tends to be the norm. After giving Ralph instructions to lean back into his harness and walk up the rock face at the same time as he was being pulled, we gave the signal and the hoisting commenced. After a few feet, we all realised that this might be a painful experience for him. The type of harness he wore was somewhat old fashioned, but very practical as the whole unit can be attached to the climber very simply without the need to lift one's feet into sealed leg loops. A single crutch strap linked to the waist belt ensures this simplicity, but sadly it also ensures that unless the wearer sits well back and leans away from the rock face, a rather painful experience ensues. And so it was for Ralph. As he was unceremoniously hoisted, he hung limply in the harness, and despite numerous attempts to persuade him to lean back and to push himself away from the rock with his legs, he took his punishment as only a man could. It looked and sounded excruciating. If this was a means of ensuring that Ralph never set foot near a crag again, I have no doubts that it was wholly successful. Martin and I climbed on top ropes to join the others at the top of the crag, and we joined forces to derig the gear and to walk Ralph and his companions round to easy ground and a pleasant descent. Though the going was easy, we couldn't help noticing that Ralph walked like a cowboy fresh off his horse! I think it's fair to say that it is extremely unlikely that we will ever have to rescue Ralph again!

Perhaps the oddest cragfast incident of all time came during a visit to the area by a group of Norwegian rescuers. They were a remorselessly entertaining crowd who drank enough beer to fill Stickle Tarn and who also, mysteriously for a bunch of supposedly fit mountaineers, smoked cigarettes incessantly. We attempted to entertain them with some dramatic training exercises such as raising and lowering stretchers above the still dark waters of Hodge Close Quarry, and a testing lower from half way up White Ghyll Crag, but we were keen to involve them on a real incident, should one arise. The opportunity came towards the end of their visit and, at first, it appeared that all the training we had been doing could come in useful, as the report was of a walker stuck near Stickle Tarn.

The phrase 'near Stickle Tarn' could suggest many alternatives, the huge rock faces of Pavey Ark or lesser but potentially awkward cliffs on the flanks of Harrison Stickle and just beneath the rim of the corrie on Tarn Crag. A huge crowd of rescuers – perhaps a record – set out to rendezvous at the outflow of the tarn, so many in fact that the path up Stickle Ghyll looked very much as it does on a busy summer day. With enough rescuers to form a human pyramid tall enough to snatch a stranded walker from the highest crag in the area, we were all stunned to find the casualty not 300 feet up Pavey Ark, but lying down near the outflow to the tarn.

The situation was, in fact, as we had been informed, and the man was indeed suffering from vertigo – genuinely terrified and rooted to the spot, despite the fact that by comparison to many mountainsides, the terrain he was on was as flat as a pancake. He must have been quite amazed at having such a huge team of international rescuers at his disposal and, though the Norwegians experienced the somewhat dubious delights of carrying a stretcher down a steep Langdale fellside, we did cringe a little, as this was one of the least serious incidents we had dealt with for a long time. Though it no doubt felt serious enough to the casualty, in particular as he was being hurtled down the hill by a bunch of chain-smoking Norwegian rescuers with a very peculiar sense of humour.

6

ALL CREATURES
GREAT AND STUCK

There is a widely held belief amongst actors and other media personalities that children and animals will either upstage you or sabotage any serious attempt to involve them on stage or screen. The rampant baby elephant on *Blue Peter* springs to mind as a perfect example of this. Whilst as a rescuer I have never had the misfortune to deal with a young tusker with a broken leg, I can state without any trace of doubt that attempting to rescue animals presents one with an even wider range of problems than any found in normal human call-outs. In my experience the animals show neither gratitude, nor any sort of due regard for the rescuer's safety (something that could sometimes also be said about humans!), often deliberately attempting to wrest them from the rock face in some sort of mutual kamikaze bid. Sheep are particularly noted for this. Seemingly blessed with completely inadequate cerebral powers, they will save their last vestiges of strength for a wild thrashing attempt to hurl both rescuer and self to oblivion. Hardly the actions of an intelligent individual hoping to be safely extricated from a dangerous situation.

There is however one example I can recall in which an animal not only showed due gratitude after being rescued, but also displayed courage and strength beyond that which I would ever have thought possible, however more of that later. Many people have dogs, and many people have dogs which are unique, special and very precious. Mine was no exception, though it has to be said that it did also display a host of less savoury qualities, mostly connected with a voracious appetite and a tendency to overuse a set of fortunately blunt teeth. Apart from the normal anti-social behaviour expected from dogs of dubious pedigree – lunch boxes ripped apart, contents devoured in seconds and sandwiches snatched from unsuspecting hands – one incident remains fixed in my mind as a perfect example of the many embarrassing moments the beast caused.

I was working for the National Park Ranger Service at the time, checking the network of rights of way in the Langdale and Little Langdale areas. This often involved discussing problems with landowners and tenant farmers and attempting to find solutions which would be acceptable to all parties. On this occasion I was in Little Langdale, discussing the line of a right of way which cut through the garden of a typical slate-constructed ancient Lakeland house. As was almost always the case, I was invited inside to discuss the matter over a civilised cup of tea, whilst the 'la'al crocodile', as one local farmer had already renamed Ruffly, sat outside. However, the kitchen door had been left temptingly ajar. We discussed the problems of the path – could it be re-routed to avoid the garden, would the ramblers accept this, were there any overriding historical factors? These matters were sorted in an amicable fashion and I promised to return with some answers and some signs which would clearly indicate the correct route. Whilst we chatted, I had noted a few scuffling sounds from the kitchen, but chose to ignore them. My host showed me to the door, where the dog stood far too quietly and contentedly for my liking, licking its lips. I sensed trouble and was about to make a hasty departure when a voice behind me said, 'I'm sure I left that joint out on the side here, Bernard.' A quick backward glance revealed only a shining white plate and a trace of muddy pawmark on the worksurface.

'Bye!'

On another occasion I went to visit my long-standing climbing partner, Wilf Williamson, at Charlotte Mason College, where he worked as a chef. Fresh from preparing trout for an evening dinner, Wilf came out of the kitchens carrying a small plastic bag, which he left on a window ledge whilst we discussed plans for the next day's climbing. Soon the dog came and sat next to us, licking its lips constantly, as though it had just eaten a good curry. Wilf turned, to see the bag he had brought out for the bins open and empty. Its former contents? Two hundred trout eyes.

The National Park has a depot on the outskirts of Ambleside, near the refuse dump and the sewage works. I was sorting signs and gates out for some work projects we had, whilst the dog, as usual, chased everything that moved from bees to birds. Midway through the afternoon, I noticed that I had not seen her for a while. I shouted, and whistled, and shouted some more. Waited. Whistled and shouted again, but nothing. This was unusual as, despite her flaws, she was generally obedient and defiantly loyal. I began to search the area, concerned that we were not far from a busy road, but the searches revealed nothing. By now, I was extremely concerned and sensed that something was seriously amiss. Seagulls flew low over the tip and strutted about in the sewage works, noisy and incongruous.

The sewage works? I wondered. The gates were locked and there was no evidence of the dog being there, but some extraordinary sense led me to scramble over the tall gates and into the works. I called, but heard nothing, called again and was bitterly disappointed. I was sure the dog was here somewhere. Then I saw her. Or rather I saw the black tip of her nose, poking out of the slurry in the centre of a huge pit, whose contents were disgusting, immeasurably deep and several feet down from its retaining concrete lip. The nose disappeared. Then nothing.

For a moment I was totally stunned. I thought I had literally seen the last moment of her life and been unable to do anything to save her. The pit was quite inaccessible and unbelievably dangerous. To contemplate going in to attempt a rescue was absolutely out of the question, so I hurriedly looked around for anything which might be useful. Seconds passed so slowly, then I found an aluminium ladder lying against a building. Rushing back to the pit side, there was still no trace of the dog, but I pushed the ladder out into the slurry where I had last seen her nose. Almost immediately I felt a movement through the latter and like some terrible monster evacuating a foul swamp, the dog started to haul itself up the ladder. Slowly and deliberately, she dragged herself out of the sludge, on to the open ladder, and then up to and over the edge. Completely unrecognisable as a dog, never mind my own, she then did the one thing that all dogs do when they are wet. She shook herself. All over me.

I rushed her down to the river, which was fortunately only a few yards away and we both jumped in, probably accounting for more pollution than is normally released into Windermere in a week. Thoroughly washed, and drying in a hot afternoon sun, I reflected on the ordeal she had suffered. My guess is that she chased seagulls into the sewage works and leapt straight into the pit, tricked by the fact that the surface was thick and strong enough to take a seagull's weight, but obviously not hers. Unable to get out of the pit as its concrete sides were completely smooth and at least three feet above the level of the slurry, she had swum round and round for at least half an hour in the thick sludge. This was, I am sure, only possible due to her incredible fitness and to the hours spent swimming in local tarns and lakes. The most difficult thing to understand was the incredible draw that took me into the sewage works. It was a really powerful feeling and I am convinced that some sixth sense – call it what you will – was at work here. Though I viewed her with great affection before this event, there is no doubt in my mind that she was fully aware that I had saved her life, and in spite of the fact that she was the most cantankerous and unpredictable animal I have ever come across, there was always a very special feeling between us for the rest of her time.

I have to confess to having little sympathy for the fox-hunting fraternity. Their arguments for the continuation of hunting are often tenuous and, when all's said and done, those involved are getting their enjoyment out of their quarry's severe distress and often death. Knowing the lengths which some huntsmen will go to in order to achieve a good hunt with the right results, such as blocking holes and hiding places so the fox has to keep on running, also fails to endear them to me.

Though, in the Lake District, hunting is still carried out on foot by a few, the majority of the hunt followers use a calvacade of four-wheel drive vehicles to make things easier, watching the proceedings through binoculars from the nearest road or navigable track. If the fox happens to disappear over a ridge into the next valley, the whole fleet has to attempt to follow, normally causing traffic problems more usually associated with the M6 on a bank holiday. The already narrow roads become almost impassable at times, and any attempt to force a way through is met with an intimidating scrutiny. Are you one of us or one of them? question the stares.

My strongest personal experience of hunting occurred recently in Tilberthwaite, when I was positioned above the famous ghyll which rushes down from Wetherlam. It is usually the frantic baying of the hounds which alerts the casual observer to their presence, as they can be difficult to spot on large complex fellsides, but on this occasion, I saw them easily, strung out in a line and covering the rough fell and scattered woodland at breakneck speed. Their course took them along the side of Holme Fell, through the oak woods and then towards the ghyll. Suddenly, not a hundred yards away, I spotted the fox, a beautiful creature with rich brown flanks and a paler fawn-coloured tail. It ran up through the steep intake fields directly opposite us, tiring as it ascended, with the hounds closing fast, not fifty yards behind. Its end looked certain as it headed for a corner of high walls and we feared the worst, but as the hounds' baying reached a crescendo, the fox disappeared, confusing the pack leaders. Hounds leapt walls and scoured a huge area in seconds for the scent, but the wily fox had temporarily at least given them the slip. It appeared momentarily a short time later, higher on the fellside, but by now the hounds were back on its trail. The incident only lasted a few short minutes, but my lasting memory is of an intense feeling of the terror which the fox must have felt as the hounds closed in on it in the corner of the field. At that moment the cruelty and suffering taking place was so openly displayed I could feel little more than contempt for those who were equally blatantly enjoying every minute of it.

However, despite any ill-feelings I may harbour towards the hunting fraternity in general, it is difficult to extend this feeling directly to the hounds, and on two occasions, foxhounds have been the subject of intriguing yet quite different rescues.

The first instance occurred in Dovedale, one of Lakeland's most impressive valleys. Deeply carved and with an ever steepening headwall crowned by the magnificent Dove Crag, the dale is often quiet outside weekends in the winter, and so it was one frosty December morning when I set out with a client to climb one of Dove's fine gullies. A bitter easterly wind had left excess drainage water frozen like ancient larva flows across the path and in places crampons were a necessity rather than a luxury. I first heard the faint, distant howling about a mile or so from the crag, although by now the wind swirled from every direction and the source of the noise was uncertain. As we gained height towards the crag, the howling intensified, varying between a baleful moaning and a chilling baying which made the hounds of the Baskervilles sound like ageing pekineses. Though reason dictated that the source of the noise was canine, I have to confess that the chill swirling mist, coupled with merely a modicum of imagination, gave rise to images of an altogether more sinister nature. The final short distance to the foot of the crag was truly memorable. It sounded as though we were surrounded by fearsome howling beasts, as the wind whipped and slung the terrible sounds around the dark buttresses which towered above us. Only at the very last minute did the source become apparent, as we scrambled across the jumbled blocks at the base of the crag and realised that it came from beneath our feet. Many bigger Lakeland crags have long run outs of scree beneath them, remnants of the retreat of the Ice Age and subsequent erosion. A few have notable areas in which the blocks of scree are of a huge size, and as they have fallen to rest over the years, so this has created hollows and tunnels beneath which provide ideal natural shelters, locally known as 'borrans'. This rocky borrans represented one of the finest I had seen in the region. Providing natural cover for fox, even badger and rabbit at lower levels, this particular one had become a potential tomb for a foxhound whose quarry, pack and owner were long gone.

Carefully picking my way across the rime-encrusted boulders, brushing light powder snow off and carefully peering into the murky crevices beneath, I finally located the dog. The speed with which my proffered sandwich was devoured confirmed its hungry state, but though food could be dropped freely and we could easily have reached down and stroked its head, had we not been concerned that in the dark our hands may have looked like an inviting sandwich, the holes in this rocky labyrinth were simply too small for the hound to escape and the rocks too large to move. As it paced anxiously beneath us, desperate to escape a premature burial, we eventually located what looked like an escape passage, but the hound would not be enticed to the same spot. There was only one thing for it. Reluctantly, we tore up our sandwiches into treat-sized lumps and started leading a trail through the complex subterranean passages, using the sandwiches as bait. Dropping the food at strategic points resulted in the hound literally eating his way to safety, and after several minutes of intricate route-finding and blind alleys he surfaced, pathetically scrawny, blinked a few times in the bright mist and promptly ate the rest of our dinner without even asking! With the weather closing in we opted to descend with the dog in tow, whereupon we befriended it until half a mile before the farm, where it raced off without a backward glance or a bark of gratitude.

More recently, the phone rang one Sunday morning.

'John, it's Keith. Wiv a 'ound fast on a benk under t'Long Top, can y'ev a do at it.'

Aware of the normal inexactitude of Keith's descriptions and of the huge area of rock beneath Crinkle Crags where the said 'ound was 'fast', I hesitated for a moment before agreeing to go up and attempt a rescue if someone who knew its exact whereabouts would tag along. Keith's eldest son, Bruce, and the dog's owner would be my companions. Armed with a thin 55-metre rope and some abseiling gear, we began the long trek up from Oxendale via Whorneyside Breast to the coves of Crinkle Crags.

The way along Oxendale bottom is pleasant, with only the gentlest of rises and the grandest of Lakeland views onto Pike O'Blisco and the rolling crest of the Crinkles. However, once the footbridge at the foot of Whorneyside beck is reached, the character of the walk alters most unsubtly. Ahead lies a long arduous plod up a broad rounded breast of land which is at the same time steep and unforgiving. We spoke briefly and intermittently, each person afraid to admit to any breathlessness or sign of fatigue, despite a pace which would have left most fell walkers way behind. After all, climbers, farmers and huntsmen would never want to concede inferior fitness to each other, each mistakenly believing themselves to be masters of the open fellsides. The steep grass and bracken gradually gave way to grass and herbs, grass and scree, then scree and boulder, heralding the last few hundred feet to the foot of the crags. Suddenly we heard the hound, its rough bark echoing around the windless coves. Unlike many of the sheep which become stuck on these crags, the hound was fortunately easy to spot, though this was little consolation as we studied its precarious perch. The first thing which occurred to me was to question how the dog had been able to get into such an exposed, difficult and dangerous location without ending up in a heap at the foot of the crags. A full 160 feet up, it sat on a ledge just three feet long and two feet deep, with no obvious access route from above, below or to the side. It had the appearance of having been placed there by winch from a helicopter and told to stay put. To compound things further, the dog's owner insisted that I needed to take a smelly old rag and his sandwiches in order to settle its aggressive tendencies to an extent which would allow me to harness it up and abseil back down to safety. I have to admit that it seemed that it would take more than sandwiches and rags to do this.

Bruce and the dog's master waited disbelievingly as I scrambled up a loose gully towards a vague line of ledges which ran out towards the hound. A few loose stones whistled down towards them, emphasising the seriousness of the situation and encouraging their speedy evacuation from the foot of the crag to a safer area, as I had already advised. One hundred feet higher, the traverse line was painfully obvious. A series of sloping rock ledges, some black-carpeted with lichen, others lush with bilberry and heather, led away from the safe confines of the narrow gully in which I was comfortably ensconced. Each step of the traverse would increase the exposure, the climber's term for the sense of fear which the height creates, and it was no place for a slip. As with all climbing, the main way of dealing with the fear is to concentrate fully on the immediate task in hand. Feet are placed with micrometer precision, each handhold caressed until the optimum grip is found, total focus on the immediate surroundings, whilst the drop below and the fear remain blurred and background.

This particular piece of climbing was by no means difficult, though the uncertainty associated with unfamiliar terrain and slippery rock lent an air of seriousness to the situation, enhanced by the fact that I was having to climb solo, without protection, and that at the far end of the traverse awaited a bad-tempered hound with sharp teeth. A few minutes later I stood, or rather clung, just feet from the dog. It growled and bared its teeth, which was all the encouragement I needed to climb above it to search for a suitable anchor point from which to abseil. Previous experience with lively Herdwick sheep had taught me the absolute necessity of always ensuring that animal rescues in dangerous situations are carried out with the rescuer firmly attached to something and, fortunately, a large spike of rock above and just to the side of the hound's ledge provided a superb belay. The rope snaked down to the foot of the crag, the knot in its end brushing the ground (I've always tied a knot in the end of the rope since a friend of mine slid off the end of his in the dark, blissfully unaware that it was twenty feet short of the bottom). As the rope was very thin, I arranged a special abseiling system on my harness to increase the friction and set off gently down to make the acquaintance of my canine friend.

I locked off my abseiling device so that I was secure on the ledge system a couple of metres to the side of the dog's location, and edged my way gingerly across, well aware that if I frightened him and caused a slip, his lack of wings would be a distinct disadvantage. I made all the usual calming noises that one makes in situations such as this – 'Hello, boy, good lad' – and so on, and realised that to have remembered his name would have been a useful start. Edging closer, it was clear that he was extremely anxious, no doubt partially due to the fact that I did not resemble one of his hunting masters. A long deep growl confirmed this, and it was extremely difficult to construe the drawn jowls and bared teeth as a friendly smile.

I spent a few moments envisaging how I would calm the hound, fasten a makeshift harness to him, clip him to the rope and abseil 160 feet to the ground, but all I came up with was a clear vision of myself abseiling as fast as possible, with the dog attached to my arm by his teeth. Just as it seemed that all might be lost as the dog backed towards oblivion, I remembered the sandwich and smelly rag in my pocket. With overdue alacrity I yanked out the rag and held it out, a sort of pipe of peace. The dog sniffed at it and seemed to settle a little. Now was surely the time for the master stroke – the sandwich. Removing the crushed offering swiftly from my pocket, I held it nervously out, and in an instant our relationship metamorphosed. I was suddenly the friend, with hands to be licked, not nipped. Shuffling across, I talked to him, praised him and fed him another sandwich, all the time manoeuvring into a position in which I hung over the edge of the crag, between him and the void.

That was the easy bit done. The next stage involved improvising a safe harness out of slings and fastening it to the dog in such a way that he would not panic and perhaps fall, and indeed that he could not slip out of during our descent. As the slings slipped gently around his chest and belly, he suddenly threw what could only be described as a classic wobbler, struggling to escape my clutches and risking a fatal fall. As I held on tight I could hear a loud gasp from the open-mouthed onlookers below, before control was regained and I was able to tighten the slings and clip him to the rope via a jumar clamp.

Now for the moment of truth. I re-attached him to my harness and released him from the rope above in readiness for the descent. Understandably, he was reluctant to leave the apparent security of the ledge and leapt about inconsolably, thrashing his head and tail about. I eased downwards, but he leapt up, claws scrabbling at the rock. More gasps from below. I decided that rougher tactics were now essential, and I'm afraid to say that as I descended further, the hound had no alternative but to follow and after a short fall, we were both suddenly hanging away from the rock, peering into each other's eyes. The abseil was mostly free from the rock, which made things considerably easier, as the hound had nothing but me to try to climb onto, and we quickly slid down to safety. Hound and owner were reunited in a blaze of smelly rags and dog biscuits and he raced to the nearby spring to slake his thirst. Broad grins all round and the final compliment from Bruce. 'Whitey,' he said, 'yer a mad bugger!'

The very last doggy incident I want to mention will serve as a warning to all owners of afghan hounds and other similarly hairy beasts. With a reasonable depth of snow lying, and a freezing level of about 1000 feet, conditions were superb for winter mountaineering and skiing, but less so for dog-walking. Called out to a snowy Easedale to rescue a dog, the team came across a most dejected afghan with a solid, football-sized lump of ice frozen to the hair on its belly. Sticky wet snow has gradually built up, snowball-fashion and as the party had gained altitude and reached the freezing level, the compressed, saturated snow had set like concrete, causing the dog eventually to keel over. Efforts to chip the ice away with a variety of sharp implements failed and the dog, complete with giant iceball, was loaded onto the stretcher and carried unceremoniously to the valley. Any passer-by lifting the protective cover would have had quite a shock! A local vet managed to thaw the ice with warm water, and the dog fortunately survived its ordeal.

The most numerous of Cumbria's mountainside inhabitants are of course sheep which, as everyone knows, do not readily conjure an image of beings of great intelligence. Not content with acting stupidly, they also have an unfortunately mindless appearance and a penchant for following other sheep lemming-like, regardless of the situation or outcome. My own involvement with sheep has been considerably more innocent than some would like to make out, though the occasion in Langdale when a small Herdwick leapt from a bank and through the open side window of my van, landing on my lap, took some explaining.

The most commonly found breeds in the Lake District are the Herdwick, reckoned to be the area's most ancient stock from times of Viking colonisation, the Rough Fell and the Swaledale. Of these, the Herdwick is probably the most unfortunate, having the appearance when sheared of a cross between a sheep, a donkey and ET. It is also the most gymnastic of sheep, leaping walls which would daunt all other stock and performing a wide variety of acrobatics to outmanoeuvre sheepdogs, much to the chagrin of the local shepherds.

They also possess an unerring ability to get into the most

awkward and desperate positions on local crags, from where rescue is normally the only alternative to tumbles which are almost certainly fatal. My first unpleasant acquaintance with a cragfast sheep came whilst climbing a famous rock climb called Astra on the East Wall of Pavey Ark. Initially climbed by Alan Austin and 'Matey' Metcalfe, Astra has a reputation for providing an intense climbing experience, with a series of unprotected, technical and delicate moves in an intimidating location leading to the original 'thank God' handhold. I had noticed a sheep grazing on a small sloping ledge high above the climb, but thought nothing of it. The route was totally absorbing. Pavey's rock is often bubbly and rough, magnificent to climb on but at times reluctant to offer larger holds and good protection. The crux of the route consists of an intricate sequence on small edges with, at the time, only a very old rusty piton for protection. After several sorties to crack the code posed by the complex moves, I finally made it, and stretching up to the right felt my fingers curl around a superb handhold. Almost at the exact same time, I heard a whistling sound, and a fine looking Herdwick dropped past me, not ten feet away, to land a hundred feet lower, smashed to a pulp by the jagged rocks in the gully bed. Whatever the reason, the same sheep we had seen earlier had decided to vacate its precarious perch, with disastrous consequences. Though the cause of great amusement after the event, it provided a sobering thought at the time and I often ponder on the effect this incident could have had on our climbing, had it happened just a few minutes earlier whilst I was still below the hard part.

Another time, above Red Dell on the Coniston Fells I was searching for evidence of peregrines on a quiet crag, perhaps a hundred feet high. As I ate my sandwiches at the foot of the scree and gazed at the dark grey buttress, I caught sight of a Herdwick leaping from a small ledge near the top of the crag. It fell initally like a skydiver without a parachute, limbs spread-eagled, for about eighty feet, before crashing into the rough scree slope. It rolled for perhaps another hundred feet down broken rock before coming to a halt. Seconds later it was back on its feet and with a quick shiver-like shake, it calmly walked to the side and re-commenced grazing.

Rescuing stranded sheep became a commonplace event during my work with the National Park, partly due to the fact that farmers thought us rangers directly responsible for any misfortune which might befall them, and partly because, as a climber, I would be able to reach any ledge on which the animals may have become fast, without having to resort to the complex lassoing techniques employed by some of them. I suspect the farmers also thought us expendable. I often pondered on exactly why and how sheep manage to attain such awkward and dangerous locations and have come to the conclusion that a number of factors are responsible. Firstly, the more difficult the location, the better the grazing and there is no doubting the attraction of sweet grass. Secondly, sheep are far more adept at jumping down than they are at climbing back up. Thus they will often descend onto ever more difficult terrain as a direct result of not being able to re-ascend each time. Lastly, one has to question their sanity. What else other than a sheep would reappear on the same preposterously positioned ledge just hours after being rescued?

Preventative methods have been tried. Many crags have short sections of wall in places where it seems to serve no useful purpose whatsoever. These may have been built many years ago to prevent access to ledge systems upon which sheep would normally become stuck. Several farmers have introduced goats to the fellsides, their concept being that the goats will readily gain access to the ledges which trap the sheep, but that the goats will strip the ledges of grass and herbs, so rendering them unattractive to anything else. This is fine in theory, but it has two major drawbacks. Firstly, the goats are not selective enough in their grazing, and also enjoy vertiginous, sheep-free locations where rare plants are found – or rather they used to be found before the goats ate them all. And secondly, it just does not seem to work, as the sheep still become fast.

I have probably carried out fifty or so sheep rescues over the years. The largest number of sheep rescued at the same time from the same cliff stands at five, an unusual event which occurred in Far Easedale. The farmer at Brimmer Head, Philip Powell, rang me to request assistance. Only at the end of the conversation, after I had agreed to help, did he mention that there were so many. I'm certain I could hear sniggering in the background! The gauntlet had been laid down.

I turned up in the farmyard with my trusty companion and fellow-climber, Wilf Williamson. Philip was busy doing something unspeakable (but not *that* unspeakable) with his lambs, but on spying us, he rushed across and gleefully briefed us on the current situation. Yes, there were indeed five of his best ewes stuck on the crag. However, a sixth had already fallen, and was 'badly' with internal injuries. 'Ye'll need this,' exclaimed Philip with a knowing smile as he handed us an old rag. Wrapped inside was a knife with which we were to cut the throat of the poor sheep. Wilf and I looked at each other as I assessed the sharpness of the blade. Who would do the deed? Would we be able to do the deed? As we left the farmyard and walked towards the bridlepath which would lead us to Deer Bield Crag above the lonely valley of Far Easedale, the conversation was stilted, morbid. It transpired that neither of us had the ruthlessness required to slit the animal's throat. We discussed dropping large boulders on it and various other means of effecting the same end result, but all seemed as bad as each other.

With the knife temporarily tucked out of sight and mind in the top of my rucsac, we enjoyed a fine walk into Far Easedale. Less frequented and with a more desolate atmosphere than its immediate and immensely popular neighbour, Easedale, the valley rises gently via an ancient bridlepath, then a wet trod which passes beneath the foreboding mass of Deer Bields. The crag faces north-east, so attracts little sun, but plentiful quantities of moss and lichen streak the rock with varying shades of green and grey, some of which appear luminescent after periods of rain. The rock itself is compact and tends to give either 'good 'ods or bugger all', as one climber put it, quite different to many Lakeland rock types which give a plentiful supply of holds. Despite these disappointing factors, determined pioneers have created some quite excellent climbs here. The left-hand side of the cliff is split by a dark gash known as Deer Bield Crack. First ascended in February 1930, the crux pitch consists of a formidable narrowing chimney which an old guidebook describes as 'unique of its type' and requiring 'considerable energy and perseverance'. Like an hourglass, the exit from the chimney pitch not only narrows but also forces the climber outwards to its very edge, demanding a thrutching technique to achieve success, in which knees, elbows and virtually everything else you care to mention is used to maintain upwards progress. Nearby, the main crag has long sported a classic route, Deer Bield Buttress. The upper part of the route was loose for some time and, though no surprise, it was nonetheless a sad moment when the top pitch disappeared and the climb changed forever as a result of a huge rockfall in the early 'eighties, probably caused by a small earth tremor. The massive slabs of rock which lie on the scree beneath the cliff bear testimony to this event.

One final climb here worth recalling is Peals Before Swine, a delicate route climbed as one 160-foot (50m) run out and graded E3. This bold and sustained pitch with sparse protection and a serious feel gave me one of the most intense climbing experiences I can ever remember. Though I was climbing with Paul Cornforth, an extremely fit young climber who had undeniably superior skills, I somehow ended up at the sharp end. The rock was dusty and had a heavy growth of moss and lichen which made it appear that the route had not been ascended for many months. Around the half way mark comes the most worrying part of the ascent, and although the hardest piece of climbing has already been disposed of at this stage, it remains difficult and extremely precarious, a situation exacerbated by the lack of any satisfactory protection. I can clearly recall clinging to inadequate fingerholds whilst my feet slid inexorably downwards on sloping rock as the dirt and lichen ground like fine ball bearings beneath the smooth rubber of my climbing shoes. As each foot slipped, I would gently replace the other like a slow motion treadmill before realising that this resolution to the predicament was likely to be anything but permanent. A few more moves, carried out by instinct and blind panic rather than rational judgement, brought a good resting hold and a nut placement which offered instant security. It is impossible to describe the intensity of the moment at a time like that. Maybe it's a bit like a tangled parachute suddenly opening and transforming a potentially fatal situation into one of real security. What I do recall clearly is saying to myself over and over again that I was giving up climbing. That was twelve years ago and it hasn't happened yet! In fact, some of the enjoyment in climbing can be found in retrospective analysis. At the time, the climb can seem so frightening and unpleasant that you might think it your last, but once completed, things never seem quite as bad. Later, in the pub, it might become a fine route, well worth doing and a month later it could easily have become one of the great classics. Such is the mind's ability to concentrate on the good memories and bury the bad!

Fortunately for us, the main cliff was not to be on the agenda for today as the stranded sheep were distributed randomly on a huge vegetated buttress to the right of the main climbing area. We could clearly see them, their creamy white fleeces starkly obvious against the dark greys and greens of the cliff. Seeing them was one thing, evacuating them all safely would be another matter completely. But first, we had some business to take care of which involved the use of a not very sharp knife. At this point I have to admit that neither of us was prepared for the supposed act of mercy which we had been asked to carry out, and alternative methods of effecting the same result were still being discussed on the ascent to the base of the crag, which was considerably slower paced than normal, not only due to the large amount of equipment we carried. The favoured method was fast becoming established as the use of a large rock. Then we saw it, seventy or eighty yards away, lying apparently contentedly on a grassy patch at the cliff base, exactly where Philip had described it. I had already envisaged trying to hack a way through the thick fleece and skin with our blunt knife, and the probable mess which a spurting jugular would create, but the thoughts led nowhere and it seemed than no amount of imagery and mental preparation would equip us for the deed. Withdrawing the knife from its protective rag, we steeled ourselves for what had to be done and purposefully approached the ewe, which lay with its head turned away as if wanting to remain ignorant of our advance. When we got to her, though she looked alive and well even from a short distance, she was in fact stone dead. Phew!

We decided to rescue the sheep from above. Three ewes were trapped in a fairly tight area, perhaps half way down a 200-foot section of steep rock, rippled with bounteous ledges of bilberry and heather, whilst another two were fast on the edge of a loose and vegetated gully, about fifty feet from the ground, but a long way from the access point at the crag top.

Things started disastrously. The first ewe was in the most difficult location, trapped on a slim rock ledge which slanted at a steep angle downwards and outwards, narrowing at its end to a point from which there was nowhere to go but down – and fast. Following the same technique as adopted for the cragfast hound, I abseiled down just to one side until beneath the stranded sheep, then re-ascended in order to force it up the ledge and tackling it, rugby-fashion, if it either attempted to re-ascend, or make a dash to descend past me. This technique is usually successful, though it demands a positive attitude and no small amount of strength. On this occasion, we were to be surprised. Before I had reached the ledge on which the poor beast was fast, it ran to the edge and without a moment's hesitation jumped. The logical conclusion to be drawn at this point was that it had sealed its fate most effectively, but a surprise was still in store. Some way down from its launch pad a gnarly old rowan tree grew out from a bilberry-clad ledge. The ewe hit a horizontal branch and revolved a full acrobatic circle which would have done Olga Korbut proud, before falling again onto a further ledge and then the scree. It got up and walked away as though nothing had happened.

The next two went relatively smoothly. Both were caught easily, no doubt tired from days spent with limited food and water on their captive ledges, but carrying them eighty feet or so back up the cliff was no easy matter. My technique was to encircle them tightly with slings, then attach them to the main rope with a sliding jumar clamp, which can be moved up the rope, but which will not slide down. Climbing ledge to ledge, the sheep were unceremoniously hauled behind, ten feet or so at a time. Occasionally they panicked and attempted manic leaps outwards, but were restrained by the ropes. Finally, arriving exhausted at the easy ground at the top of the crag where Wilf reliably took in the slack rope, we were met by one final challenge – Ruffly. Extremely reliable on the open fells where she would not glance twice at a sheep, this was a different matter and, as we finally tried to haul the ewes to safety, we were set upon by a whirling mass of paws, teeth and fur which sent the sheep into a terrified frenzy which only abated once we were well clear of the edge of the crag and the dog was securely leashed.

The last two were satisfying simple. Wilf lowered me on a long rope and the ewes gave up with little more than a token fight. Fastening one onto each side of me, he continued lowering us the extra fifty feet or so to the ground, giving the bewildered sheep an abseiling experience which many people gladly pay good money for.

Back down at the farm we told Philip that the ewe he had asked us to kill was now dead, but did not elaborate, thus saving face and even gaining a few points. Delighted that the other five had been safely evacuated, albeit that one had only done so by virtue of a convenient tree, he led us into the kitchen for a beer and the reward, a scrawny-looking chicken which he assured us would need cooking slowly for a long time. Fortunately, he had already killed it. The obligatory lakeland terrier was booted from one side of the kitchen to the other and back several times amidst much snarling and shouting, cakes and sandwiches appeared and we were treated to genuine Lakeland hospitality the likes of which no tourist would ever see. Later, we cooked the chicken slowly and for a long time, but it remained as tough as old rubber.

Perhaps the worst cliff of all to attempt to rescue sheep from is Pavey Ark. Its sheer height, coupled with a complex structure and dozens of interconnecting ledges allow the sheep ample opportunity to give the rescuers a good run for their money. Many of the ledges are so spacious that it is not possible to rely on one well-known ploy to simplify things – that of leaving the animals long enough so that they are still alive, but weak from hunger. Big Herdwick ewes fast on the vastness of Pavey's ledges remain strong and agile. They cannot be tempted by handfuls of sweet grass, nor can they be lassoed from above by rope or, as one cunning farmer used to use, a long pole replete with noose. The only method left is the good old-fashioned rugby tackle, and it takes a little skill to perfect. The first and foremost rule is always to be tied on to a rope from above – if the sheep tries to leap into oblivion, the chances are it will try to take the rescuer with it. The second is always to creep round onto the ledge below and to one side, so that the sheep remains above you. Once it is beneath, the void seems to beckon them and they can easily be lost. The third stage is the most important, and involves a not inconsiderable amount of skill and timing. The sheep has to be coaxed into wanting to return down or across to the opposite end of the ledge from its present location. This may be achieved by tendering handfuls of sweet grass and dropping them at strategic locations, but this process more usually starts with subtle arm motions and common sense positioning on the ledge, and can proceed through vigorous arm-waving to throwing stones and shouting obscenities. Once it begins to move, you've got to act quickly and decisively, and rugby tackle it with the sort of conviction you would need to stop Martin Offiah in full flow. Once grabbed, it will struggle, and it has to be subdued by hanging on and holding tight until the fight has gone from it. This can take several minutes, and is best achieved by lying upon it and hoping that no one is looking. Fastening slings around it can be difficult and any momentary slackening of one's grip will result in a short but violent struggle. All you have to do then is to abseil down or haul it back up. There is one final problem which I recall becoming very apparent on one Pavey Ark rescue. It seems to be a natural reaction for the sheep to have a good pee when they feel threatened and if this happens as you make your textbook approach from below, the result does not bear dwelling upon.

7

DOWN ON THE FARM

Many years ago farmers would sometimes lend a hand in mountain rescues. They knew the area well, they were tough and resourceful and, in any case, there were few others available for the task. In more recent times, farmers are as likely to help a rescue team as they are to invite a group of French farmers round for a lamb hotpot. Lake District farmers are in many ways the same as farmers the country over – always grumbling, always working, always underpaid (they claim to be poor, everyone else claims they are wealthy!) and never wrong.

I had the sometimes dubious privilege of getting to know many of the local sheep farmers quite well as part of my work, a relationship which was always useful when rescues were taking place to facilitate vehicle access and parking, not to mention the supply of tea and cakes afterwards. In return, apart from rescuing their cragfast sheep, we might arrange for materials to be taken to locations high on the fells, courtesy of the RAF helicopters. Most of these farmers have a wealth of local knowledge, covering wildlife and historical matters, and many conversations with them are gems in their own right. What follows is just a selection of the more eccentric examples of local agricultural behaviour.

Back in the early 1980s, the Lake District still suffered from the abuse and damage created by gangs of rampaging youths. Some were so-called Hell's Angels, others were neatly dressed and drove normal cars. Whatever their appearance, their respect for property and land was often non-existent and, as the Police would only intervene in cases where damage or disturbance was caused, it was often down to the National Park Rangers to tackle these problems head-on before things deteriorated to a level at which Police involvement became necessary. Unfortunately, it was our service towards which much of the farmer's anger was generated. Why hadn't we done something about the forty Hell's Angels who had just barbecued two fine ewes, for example, as if a question like that requires a sensible answer!

It was Spider Penman who first introduced me to the techniques required for dealing with such a situation. Following a series of incidents in the Rydal Caves area, involving gangs of motorcyclists, where drugs were being freely used, needles left lying around and a heron barbecued for an evening snack, Spider and I paid the gang a visit early one morning. He was armed with only a disarming attitude and a bundle of black bin liners. We went round from tent to tent, to be confronted by bleary-eyed individuals with hangovers so severe we would have been back in our van and half a mile away before they would have been able to crawl out of their sleeping bags. Our message was simple. They weren't allowed to camp there, but we could recommend another location where they would not get moved on or harassed and, although there were no herons to roast, at least they would be able to enjoy their own form of recreation undisturbed. Our last words were, 'Here's a bin liner. Please put all your rubbish in here and leave it by the wall. Thanks.' Almost unbelievably, they were gone by lunch time and all their rubbish was neatly stacked in black bin liners.

This became standard technique for dealing with the less savoury gangs which roamed the area in busy periods, and it worked perfectly most of the time. The gangs got used to us calling round, and seemed to prefer our laid back approach to the sometimes heavy-handed attitude of the Police. All went well for a number of years, but the number of locations we could offer as alternatives diminished steadily, until we were left with one major overspill area, a windswept field high on the Walna Scar road above Coniston. This in turn often overspilled onto the open fell land nearby, which was farmed by a tough and uncompromising character whose face was chiselled like a square cut lump of grey slate. Tall and lean, and dressed as only farmers can, he cut a menacing figure, but it was when he spoke that you really stood up and noticed. His accent was Cumbrian, his manner brusque and each word spoken with a crispness which stung and a force which could wither.

My first encounter with him came after a gang of bikers had demolished his new sheepfolds and burnt them for firewood. Furious was a major understatement, and he insisted on telephoning the head of the whole National Park Service and persuaded him to come to see the damage, so that he could vent his anger on someone as high as possible within the organisation, just for the fun of it. Unbeknown to us at the time, the real fun had been taking, and continued to take place up on the fellsides. In response to this deed and others of a similar nature, he decided to take a less compromising stance than we had, regardless of the strength of the opposition.

It appeared that once the bikers had their fire burning nicely, with the kettle whistling satisfyingly on top, whatever peace the evening had was shattered as the kettle was blasted from its perch by a double-barrelled shotgun. This served as a suitable warning. On another occasion, after a heavy night's drinking during which the bikers caused yet further damage, our avenging shepherd crept round every tent and removed as many pairs of motorcycling boots as he could lay his hands on, returning them only after the damage had been paid for in full. The final and possibly most unarguable display of farmer power came when he confronted the throng of leather-clad troublemakers on his tractor. What made the instance particularly special was that one very expensive motorcycle lay balanced on his front-loader fifteen feet in the air.

The ranger for the area, Peter Farrand, and I found it hard to believe all these stories, and wondered why he had never landed himself in real trouble with these gangs who, after all, outnumbered him heavily. I discovered the probable answer myself, at first hand when I came across a group of about fifteen bikers camped on the edge of his land. Like a rather scruffy, yet more menacing version of Clint Eastwood, our farmer friend strode across towards the gang who turned and glared at him en masse. I kept a respectful distance – it was important that someone was there to call for an ambulance . . . They were a really rough looking bunch, with filthy leathers, unkempt hair and a distinctly aggressive appearance. He stood in the centre of them, looked around and issued a challenge.

'Right then, who's gan tae tak me on, lads?' I looked away. I heard his voice again. 'Come on then, there's plenty of yer tae choose frae.' Not one of them moved. 'Right then, get this mess cleared up and bugger off!' And they did just that! At that point I realised what a gamble he had taken, for a gamble it surely was. Had any one of the group taken the first step towards violence, the rest would have surely followed, and he could have been seriously hurt, but the brazen nature of his verbal assault and his daunting appearance prevented that situation from ever arising.

Another farmer with a reputation for taking a serious dislike to any tourist who strayed beyond the confines of the public footpath network was based at Rydal. He was a large man, and his reputation was such that even if the hordes of cur dogs which roamed the farmyard didn't bite your ankles, you felt certain that he would. One visitor felt his wrath at first hand. After a confrontation over a picnic site, during which both parties claimed diametrically opposing rights, the argument was settled when the holidaymaker was hoisted unceremoniously into the beck.

Instances such as this are becoming rarer now, as farmers have realised that there is gold in them thar hills in the form of tourism.

Only a few farms nowadays reject the tourist. Most welcome them in for tea and cakes, offer them B&B or a stay in their nearby holiday cottage. Some make the major part of their living from tourism and not from agriculture, the farm serving as a part of the attraction. Farms also host many of the famous Lakeland shows and nowadays may form part of tourist attractions promoted by the National Trust or National Park, offering the opportunity to see sheep-gathering demonstrations, dipping or clipping. My favourite valley for farmers is Langdale, perhaps because I know the area best, but also because of the fascinating characters who live there.

There aren't many farmers in the Lake District for example who used to belong to teddy boy gangs in Manchester. Langdale has one. A one-off in every sense of the word, Mike came to work in the area to be with his wife, who hails from Elterwater, and ended up farming the rough fell beneath the Langdale Pikes. Mike is the fortunate possessor of a wit you could cut a carpet with, and his interests outside farming separate him from almost every other farmer in the area. Sailing, hill walking for pleasure, squash, holidays in the sun and skiing have no part to play in the lifestyle of the conventional Lakeland shepherd, but Mike does them all. I can remember him coming skiing to Aviemore with a small group many years ago in conditions which would have been classed as bad in an Antarctic winter. My lasting memory of this trip is of Mike hanging onto one of the button tow lifts, getting dragged up the slope by his arms, instead of sitting on it, with his long shepherd's coat billowing out behind. Nor was this his first trip to the Cairngorms. Many years previously, he had been a keen mountaineer, and tested a tent for Don Whillans up in the northern corries in foul-weather conditions. This is a massive contradiction in lifestyle and background compared with the traditional fell farmer who has been born and bred in the valley, and for whom a trip to Lancaster would be a major event. One farmer's wife from Grasmere was talking to a group of us after a rescue, and asked one of the lads where he was from. 'Kendal,' he replied. 'Ooh, you're not going all the way back there tonight are you?' exclaimed the lady, genuinely shocked that he might be contemplating a journey of half an hour after 9.00 pm!

Perhaps the most infamous incident in recent times in Langdale has been the farcical goings on relating to the valley's annual show. Chapel Stile has hosted a gala for many years every June. It's a low-key, local and informal event, with a short fell race, stalls and competitions, sheep, dogs and pets, ice creams, all kept on time and in check by a sharp, Cumbrian announcer. Several years ago a farmer from the head of the valley, Keith Rowand, decided to hold an additional, later show at Stool End, a Lakeland Day, which would be a major event aimed at the tourist as well as the locals. These turned out to be successful shows, attracting good numbers of folk and also raising money for local charities such as mountain rescue. After a couple of good years, relationships broke down between some of those organising the event, and the following year saw two competing shows in Langdale, on the same day and not half a mile apart! Each was run by neighbouring farmers who were on opposite sides of the disagreement. Signs as far away as Windermere proclaimed the two attractions. 'Lakeland Day Show at Stool End Farm' shouted some, whilst others boasted of the 'Langdale Country Fair' at Millbeck Farm. Driving into Langdale, one was assailed by a variety of roughly painted signs, each competing to draw the visitor to their respective attraction. It ended of course in chaos, with Millbeck Farm victor in terms of visitor numbers, as it was the first show visitors reach on their way down Langdale. Only those who persevered past the well-organised marshalls, trying to draw the crowds into Millbeck, landed at Stool End. To an outsider, the situation must have seemed ludicrous and wasteful, to those who live in Langdale it was probably ludicrous, wasteful and also rather amusing. From that point on, two shows have become the norm, but fortunately the organisers have at least had the common sense to organise them on different days! This rivalry is by no means exceptional. In recent years neighbouring farmers have waged war against one another, with gates being left open to mix up stock deliberately, and the odd punch up has also been noted. The very latest saga in Langdale is a battle between the National Trust and one of its tenants who has released a herd of cows into a major Trust car park with somewhat predictable results. The cattle do what they have to do beneath the Trust's expensive new shelter and information point and there's a limit to what any self-respecting walker is prepared to acquire between the cleats of his or her boot soles!

8

A BIT HARD
FOR THE GRADE

Langdale has always been one of the premier mountain centres in Britain, providing high quality climbing and walking which can be as pedestrian or as intoxicatingly stimulating as required, yet which is always and exclusively of a highly spectacular nature. Indeed mountaineering here started many years ago and the Lake District is rightly recognised as the birthplace of British rock climbing, the great gullies and chasms on Scafell and the Wasdale fells being the cradle from which modern rock climbing evolved.

The early rock climbers were from wealthy backgrounds, for it was only they who could afford to travel and stay in such salubrious surroundings as provided by the Wasdale Head Hotel and the Old Dungeon Ghyll. They were motivated generally either by a desire to train for climbing in the Alps, then in the middle of its so-called Golden Age when virgin summits and hundreds of new routes were there for the taking, or by a desire to find an interesting route to the top of a Lakeland peak. Popular locations included Pillar Rock and the Scafell massif, where pinnacled summits could only be reached by climbing, giving a more general reason for the climb than the beauty of the climb itself.

Pillar Rock was the first summit to give what could be termed a real rock climb. The Pillar Stone, as it was known then, had attracted attention for many years and it doubtless inspired and fascinated many of the early tourists and writers, also gaining notoriety from its erroneous inclusion as the scene of the accident which provided the idea for Wordsworth's poem 'The Brothers', published in 1800. Its first ascent was a landmark which sowed the seed of English rock climbing as the sport parted company with more conventional mountaineering, which merely pursued the easiest route to the summit. The ascent was made by John Atkinson of Croftfoot, Ennerdale, and his ascent on 9th July 1826 was given due recognition in the local newspapers, one of which wrote, 'tho' the undertaking had been attempted by thousands, it was always relinquished as hopeless.' Although this may have been something of an overstatement, it is clear that the rock had a big reputation.

Three other shepherds followed his route in the same year, but it was to be twenty-two years before the next recorded ascent which was by a group of 'tourists' rather than locals. One member of this ascent party stated that he had found a bottle on top, 'containing a paper recording the names of previous visitors'. Unfortunately, he did not state their names. In 1837, *Penny* magazine stated that shepherds knew a way of getting from Mickledore on to Scafell's Broad Stand, though this was later described as 'a pleasant bit of mountain practice and nothing more'. Activity on Gable, Pillar and Scafell continued at an increased and enthusiastic rate, with the landmark ascents of Napes Needle in 1886, solo, by W. P. Haskett Smith, Eagle's Nest Ridge Direct (not an easy climb even by today's standards) by G. A. Solly in 1892, Walker's Gully on Pillar in 1899, Kern Knotts Crack by the inimitable O. G. Jones in 1897 (Though named Owen Glynne, his initials also stood for Only Genuine) and Fred Botterill's awesome ascent of the slab which bears his name on Scafell in 1903.

In Langdale, summits such as Pillar or the Pinnacle on Scafell did not exist, and many of the high crags appeared too smooth and exposed for the early pioneers, many of whom were still entrenched in the 'gully epoch' of climbing, in which they sought the security offered in cracks, chimneys and gullies. Jack's Rake on Pavey Ark was almost inevitably Langdale's first recorded climb, ascended some time in the 1870s by R. Pendlebury. This was followed by ascents in the 1880s of the Pavey Ark gullies (Great and Little), North-West Gully on Gimmer and the North Gully on Bowfell Buttress, though the only one of these Haskett Smith routes to retain any popularity is the Great Gully on Pavey Ark. Langdale lagged behind other regions at this stage, and it was only when climbers grew bold enough to tackle the blanker slabs and walls – the next era of climbing development – that Langdale really came into its own. By 1938, Gimmer Crag, Pavey Ark, White Ghyll and Bowfell had been thoroughly explored and classic routes such as Gimmer Crack and Deer Bield Crack in Far Easedale provided hard routes at the limit of what was achievable at the time.

How times have changed over the years! From revelling in the forefront of climbing development in the 'thirties, 'forties and 'fifties, Langdale's importance in the climbing world has waxed and waned, until more recently its position as a leading modern rock climbing centre has been eclipsed by many other more fashionable areas. In the 1970s high-level crags such as Gimmer and Pavey Ark were immensely popular, and were still providing high-quality new routes for those with sufficient imagination, skill and energy. However, during the 'eighties and 'nineties, development in Langdale rock climbing could not keep pace with the developments happening in the Peak District, Yorkshire, North Wales and elsewhere. True, some fine new routes were added and some worthwhile discoveries made, but in truth, the nature of the rock in Langdale by and large precludes routes of the highest modern standards. Crags are simply not steep enough, there are too many holds, and precious few big lines remain to be climbed.

In this period a massive change was taking place in the very nature of climbing and of climbers themselves. In traditional rock climbing the lead climber places protection which is removed by the second, leaving no trace of it having been there. This convention has slowly been usurped by a demand for safer and more convenient methods of climbing. Rather than have to rely on the wily skills and judgement of the traditional lead climber in placing protection and anchors, more recently we have seen the advent of the bolt – fixed protection which remains in place, and which can be placed wherever the fixer deems it appropriate. No wily skills required, simply clip the rope into the bolt by a short extension and you are instantly safe.

When bolts are placed frequently they eliminate most of the risk and remove those vital ingredients of judgement and mental application which would traditionally have been required for success. Bolt-protected routes have not yet reached the mountain crags, but they are found aplenty in the Lakeland quarries and on the limestone and sandstone outcrops which fringe the National Park. They offer low-risk, easy-access climbing, the McDonald's of the mountaineering world, fast food climbing which can taste good, but you know it's just not the real thing!

For Langdale, the effect of new climbing trends and a big influx of newcomers to the sport has been quite eye-opening. The great classics on the valley's best crags still attract more than their share of suitors, but many parts of the higher crags are almost neglected these days and some climbs are rapidly re-acquiring their cover of heather and grass – some consolation for the conservationists. A fine indicator of this trend would be to mention a small gun-powder-blasted face in Parrock Quarry, near Hodge Close. In the early 'eighties Wilf Williamson, Andy Tilney and I climbed several excellent, though short, climbs on these smooth slabs. They received plenty of ascents over the next few years, but the boldness of some of the moves put many climbers off. One route of particular merit was named One-Armed Bandit, because the crux section, high on the climb, was best tackled by grabbing a small tree which sprouted from a hairline fracture in the slate. Once weighted, the tree bent alarmingly downwards, mirroring the action of the old arcade machines!

In the late 1980s, a group of climbers placed bolts in all these climbs, and almost overnight it became the most popular climbing

Harrison Stickle, looking more Alpine than Langdale in October

Bowfell and Crinkle Crags, the highest peaks in the Langdale/Ambleside team's area

Lowering a stretcher

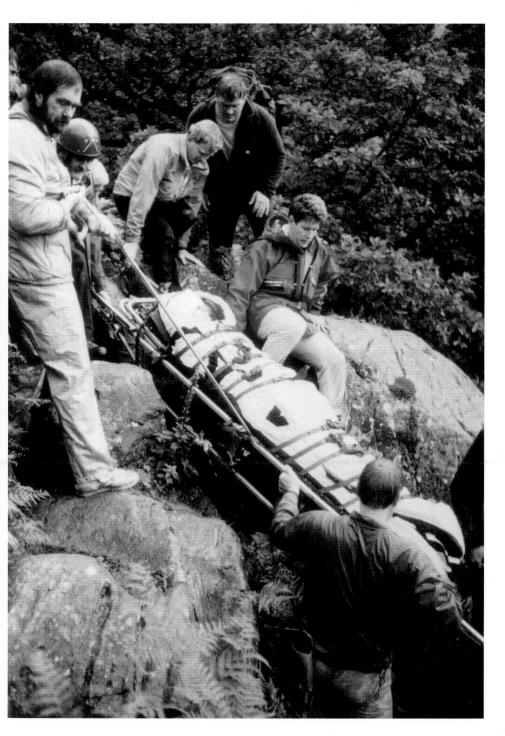

Manhandling a stretcher down awkward terrain

A typical sheep rescue

An RAF Sea King winching a casualty aboard above Striding Edge, Helvellyn

Team vehicles attending a call-out above Chapel Stile

Dr Sarah Hollis, of the Langdale/Ambleside team, carrying out first aid on a casualty

Lowering a casualty on Side Pike

(Above) Upski-ing

The author climbing Saxon

venue in the southern Lake District. Climbers wanted this style of climbing and there are now many popular locations where they can find it, including some huge indoor climbing walls. Easier routes on the traditional cliffs remain popular, evidence of the plethora of newcomers to the sport, a higher percentage of which are women than ever before. So, we reach 1996, and climbing has reached a fascinating stage in its development as a sport. Split between what many refer to as traditional climbing (though it is really unfair to deem it such – normal climbing would be a more appropriate phrase to use), and the desire for safe, bolt-protected climbs, those active in the sport have a choice to make which has significant potential impact on safety and rescue. Should climbing be maintained as it has existed, in the 'traditional' sense, without the use of fixed gear, or should the new generations of climbers fix protection points and anchors all over the routes which currently do not have them, breaking with tradition and bringing us in line with many European countries which have fixed bolts in profusion? The climbing community appears split, but generally in favour of maintaining the current compromise in which bolts are only permitted on slate quarries and certain other crags eg. limestone, where natural protection is extremely scarce. Maybe an EEC directive would help . . . maybe not!

As far as safety and rescue goes, the use of bolts on a wider scale than at present would be worrying, as their presence lends an air of security which could be misleading. Who puts them in, who maintains them? Take a recent example in the Peak District when a well-known and extremely good climber was injured when he was repeating a hard new climb which had just been bolt-protected. He leaned back on one of the bolts to have a rest and it pulled straight out. The subsequent bolts which should have held him also ripped out, resulting in a 'desmond decker' which left him with back and other injuries. Other bolts that had been placed at the same time were found to be similarly loose, a probable result of the resin which seals the twin stems of the U shaped bolt in the rock either having failed to harden or having not been added in

the first place. Although the British Mountaineering Council pro-
motes an attitude of not trusting fixed protection until you have
checked it, this can be impractical on harder routes, where there
has to be some reliance and trust on the fixing process. So a
widespread use of bolts would always present this fear.

Accidents on the bolt-protected climbing areas locally have been
very rare indeed, the biggest risk is that on slate the whole crag
will fall down. One of the problems with trying to protect climbs
on slate is that the rock is weak, and cracks into which wedges and
expanding cams can be placed may look good, but may be
dangerously insecure. A Penrith climber fell almost the full length
of the main Hodge Close cliff, ripping out his protection points
during the fall – classic 'unzipping' – and only being held by his
last placement, missing the ground by a few feet after his hundred-
foot plus plunge.

There have been some huge rockfalls in the slate quarries which
fringe the central Lake District, the latest at Hodge Close dumping
around 2500 tons of rock into the lake below, making the water
milky green with slate dust for weeks afterwards. A complete
climb disappeared in the process, and several more have disappeared over the past fifteen years as the natural cleavage lines in
the slate split great lumps off from the mother rock through the
actions of frost expansion and water lubrication. In nearby Parrock
Quarry, a group of climbs was reduced to rubble when a massive
rock slip took place. Other climbs have been left suspended from
huge slabs which are separated from the main cliff by yawning
earthy crevasses.

Most climbing accidents take place on the more traditional
climbing crags, and the reasons are many and varied. The failure
of climber-placed protection points is a common accident cause,
others include equipment failure through misuse (for example,
harness failure due to the buckle not being fastened properly),
rockfall, human error and just sheer bad luck. Unfortunately, the
nature of the sport means that mistakes may be severely punished.

One of the most embarrassing incidents I attended was at Raven

Crag, Walthwaite. This outcrop of excellent rock lies just above the village of Chapel Stile and is a popular evening crag, also used extensively for abseil training. Some years ago, along with Wilf Williamson, and my wife, Gill, I developed the right-hand part of the cliff with a number of new climbs in the HVS–E2 category. None were brilliant climbs, but all were well worth doing, and they received plenty of follow-up ascents. Just before dusk one spring evening not too much later we had a call-out to the same crag and, arriving first on the scene, I found a young climber lying against a stunted hawthorn at the foot of the crag, conscious, but with several injuries, including a possible back problem. As I assessed his condition and waited for more gear to arrive, I asked how the accident had happened, to find that he had fallen, solo-climbing, from a route just above. 'A bit hard for the grade,' was his quote at the time, and I think we both felt that there was a fine sense of irony when I told him that it was one of my routes!

This was also one of the few occasions on which a saw was required, this time to clear a couple of spiky branches which obstructed the removal of the casualty, though it must have momentarily perplexed the team members arriving in the Land Rover who could easily have thought that immediate amputation was the reason for the request! I'm glad to say that he made a good recovery, the pruning of the hawthorn was neat, and the cause of the accident could only be put down to climber error. Solo-climbing such as this finds few devotees. One mistake could be fatal, though the thrill of soloing is addictive.

Along with Wilf Williamson and a few others, I became quite hooked on solo-climbing, especially in the 1980s. Wilf and I would go to Raven Crag above the Old Dungeon Ghyll and climb fifteen or twenty climbs of between seventy and 250 feet in length in a couple of hours, whilst other conventional parties may have done just one climb. Solo-climbing is elitist and dangerous, but it represents the purest form of climbing ethic, and that adrenaline rush is quite awesome. Our solo-climbing exploits peaked with climbs such as Golden Slipper, high on Pavey Ark, Man of Straw on White Ghyll Crag and, in a rush of adrenaline and foolhardiness, a sequence of classic Extreme climbs around the sea cliffs of Devon and Cornwall and on the gritstone edges of Derbyshire, and a number of exciting Alpine climbs on the Eiger, Matterhorn and the like. I actually shudder now to look back on some of these climbs, a number of which I would not now wish to lead even with a rope! Though there are no doubt many other climbers world-wide who have climbed harder routes solo, the sense of living on the edge is the same for us all. It's the difference between the standard of the climb you're on and the standard at which you're soloing that is crucial, the closer the two are, the more intense the experience.

The other main event of our soloing exploits was an attempt to climb a hundred recognised rock climbs in the Lake District in a single twenty-four-hour period. We had climbed the magic hundred many times on smaller rock faces in the Derbyshire Peak District, but here in the Lakes, we were faced with longer climbs (the average route length we worked out at 130 feet), more awkward descents and some 'heavy beat outs' (long walks) between the cliffs.

We had earmarked a few days around midsummer for the attempt, and decided to set off one evening after tea – very much a spur of the moment decision, with no thought or preparation beforehand except that a couple of friends would help carry some bivouac gear for our few hours of slumber. We gave no thought to preparing ourselves with the right food or drink, and I seem to remember stuffing a few bars of chocolate into a bag before we departed. The weather forecast had given us a twenty-four-hour guaranteed dry slot, and previous dry conditions meant that seepage on the crags would be at a minimum, giving us dry routes to climb. We started at the Old Dungeon Ghyll at about 6 pm and headed for the well-known terrain of Raven Crag, climbing its familiar routes quickly and smoothly, sometimes down climbing to save time. A shorter climb called Mendes gave us the most trouble. Despite having climbed it before several times, it always had an atmosphere out of all proportion to its length and I don't mind saying that soloing it scared me a little.

We worked a way from left to right, climbing the Original Route, Savernake, Bilberry Buttress, Revelation, Centipede and others, then across to East Raven and Far East Raven, before descending to finish the evening's tally of thirty-three routes by climbing everything on Scout Crags. We walked steadily up to a bivouac site beneath the big sycamore tree at the foot of White Ghyll Crag, which had been very kindly prepared for us by an understanding climber friend, Andy Tilney. We snoozed until 4 am when it became just light enough to start climbing again. We did about eight routes here, before departing for Tarn Crag which lies above the path to Stickle Tarn. These were, thankfully, easy routes, but still solo-climbing, we could afford no margin of error.

The smooth flanks of Gimmer Crag were next on the list, and we decided to fix an abseil rope to make each descent easier. Gimmer Crag is positioned high on the fell above Mickleden, a huge barrel-shaped sweep of ever steepening slabs, with a complex series of ledges interconnecting to give access to the various climbs. There's a well-known old rock climbing book entitled *Space Beneath My Feet*, a description which seems quite apt when climbing on Gimmer, where even the rough heathery scree at the foot of the crag slips away so steeply, you feel 2000 feet up rather than 200, though after the event, *Space Between My Ears* would seem a more appropriate title for us. We enjoyed the Gimmer climbs immensely, but hated every bit of the dusty scree run back down to the valley, where we were fortunately met by Geoff Kirton, a kindly soul who plied us with drinks and food before we drove down to Chapel Stile to snatch four or five routes on yet another Raven Crag.

By this time, we were tiring. The hot weather and the dry dusty conditions, combined with the amount of physical and nervous energy which was being expended, was taking its toll, and an ascent of the innocuously named Route 2 felt quite daunting. Castle Rock in Thirlmere was next, and we had so far managed to climb about sixty routes. It was here that we were met by our friend Paul Allonby, a cameraman for Border TV, who were following the attempt with some interest, though you never know with news programmes whether they are interested in success or spectacular failure. We did not attempt any of the long steep climbs on the North Buttress, but instead sneaked round onto the South Buttress which has some excellent easier climbs. The hardest line we attempted here was Direct Route, an excellent VS up a striking crackline in the centre of the dome-shaped buttress, and it was here that disaster almost struck. The lower part of the climb is steep and quite strenuous and, climbing about twenty feet from the ground, the whole left-hand side of my body cramped up, from toe to fingertip. I could not hold on with my left hand, and I could not stand on my left toe, but very fortunately, my right hand was on the very best hold, and stayed there until the cramps had gone. This was a clear warning sign that the boat was now well and truly pushed out, so we put a rope on for the rest of the climb, the feeling of security oceans apart from that when we were soloing.

It's only a short hop from here to Shepherd's Crag in Borrowdale, the valley in which we hoped to complete the round. We battled through a spider's web of beginner's ropes as we climbed on autopilot up and down Brown Slabs and across to Little Chamonix. Our next route was Ardus, more strenuous and a couple of grades harder than anything we had done in the last hour, and it was here that our attempt finished and failed. More cramp, more aches and, most importantly, too much stress on our minds. To solo confidently, you need to be both physically and psychologically in tune. Running on two cylinders as we were was dangerous, and we made the decision to end the attempt then, rather than risk a potentially serious accident. We had climbed seventy-six routes and had four hours left to climb the remainder – right on schedule had we been fit enough to continue. For the record, climbs had to be completed at the rate of one ascent and descent every eight to ten minutes and we managed a total of approximately 10,000 feet of actual rock climbing, plus the walking and driving between crags. The majority of the climbs were in the V.Diff to Severe range, but with about twenty routes of VS or above. Perhaps if we had bothered to train for the attempt, or if we had paid heed to our nutritional requirements, we might have succeeded, but regardless of success or failure, we enjoyed it anyway – maybe not as much as the beer in the Britannia that evening though! I would take my hat off to anyone managing to do the full hundred. I am sure it must be possible, so if you want a list of routes – just get in touch!

Solo-climbing has claimed several lives on the Lakeland crags. The first I can remember involved a brilliant climber called John Taylor, who in the 1970s was gradually whittling away at the number of pitons which were used for aid on certain climbs. I recall meeting him with Spider Penman at the foot of a crag one day, yet only a couple of weeks later he was dead, following a fall whilst attempting to free-solo an Extreme climb called Pendulum on Deer Bield Crag. A young and popular Dave Seddon died in a fall from Raven Crag in Langdale, detailed elsewhere in this book, whilst a few others have lived to tell the tale. I must confess to having all but given up solo-climbing these days. It seems reasonable that the more you do it, the higher the odds become of something happening – a loose hold, a momentary lapse in concentration, a bit of damp rock perhaps, and in that one moment, everything can be lost.

Falls which occur whilst climbers are roped together are far more likely to have a satisfactory outcome. For the uninitiated, the lead climber carries a variety of equipment used for protection. This usually consists of a selection of metal wedges on wire or rope which can be jammed into similarly sized cracks, and some camming devices which expand to fit parallel-sided cracks in which the wedges would not grip. Wedges are generally termed nuts by climbers and camming devices are Friends, after the original manufacturer's name. The term nuts comes from the original jamming device which was a drilled out nut (as in nut and bolt) with rope threaded through it. These nuts and Friends are placed at intervals on the climb (once placed, each becomes known as a runner), the exact intervals being determined by how often suitable cracks appear and by how frightened or confident the lead climber feels.

Onlookers can often determine the lead climber's mental condition by observing the frequency and urgency with which protection is placed, especially when combined with noting the foot quiver, the wavering voice or when it gets really bad, the full body shake! If a fall does occur, the highest protection point, assuming it holds, acts like a pulley point and, providing the second climber is holding the ropes correctly through his belay device, the fall can be stopped. If a climber is ten feet above his last runner, the fall will be twenty feet plus some rope stretch and slippage, perhaps giving a twenty-five- to thirty-foot tumble.

The tremendous shock-loading which is created is dealt with by the wonderful shock-absorption properties of the rope and the fallen leader hopefully ends up safe and sound. The steeper the rock, the safer a fall is, as the climber is likely to end up hanging in space. This happened to a climber on White Ghyll Crag, whose main section fair bristles with overhangs. His fall presented him with an unfortunate problem. Hanging in space beneath the overhang, he was unable to get back on to the rock to continue the climb, the distance to the ground was too great for him to be lowered all the way, and he was unable to climb the rope using prussik knots. The team were called to assist, and it was Spider who abseiled down to extricate the embarrassed climber from his predicament. Sadly, his appearance was not as gratefully received as one might imagine, for the climber told Spider in no uncertain terms that he did not require rescuing, and would he please go away. After a reasonable exchange of views, the climber changed his mind and the rescue took place in a relatively simple fashion. The climber probably had heart failure when Spider produced a very sharp knife and cut his rope, though it must be stressed that he had attached the climber to an abseil rope beforehand!

White Ghyll Crag has been the scene of several quite nasty incidents, most of which seem to have involved loose rock. That was certainly the case when a young climber fell from the Inferno area of the crag, landing on the rough screes and sustaining terrible injuries to his wrist, along with other, potentially life-threatening complications. The rescue operation involved some difficult first aid, both in terms of life support and minimising the long term damage to his wrist. The evacuation down the steep scree and broken rock to a point from where the helicopter could winch was achieved by creating a continuously moving human conveyor belt, which gently passed the stretcher from outstretched arm to outstretched arm, while those at the back raced down to the front to maintain the cycle. Some time later, during the filming of a programme on mountain rescue for Channel 4, the climber involved, Neil, came down to the Old Dungeon Ghyll to take part in some informal filming. His wrist was encased in a metal frame, with pins literally staking his arm and hand in the correct position. Though it looked pretty grim, he was in fact making good progress and it was heartening to see the team's work showing such positive results.

There are probably more Raven Crags in the Lake District than any other, though there are several Black Crags, Rough Crags, Eagle and Falcon Crags, amongst others. In Langdale, there is a Raven Crag above Chapel Stile and another, more popular one, above the Old Dungeon Ghyll. This particular one extends a considerable distance towards the New Hotel, and has been sub-divided into Raven Crag, East Raven Crag, Far East Raven Crag and, believe it or not, Very Far East Raven Crag. The main buttresses provide excellent easily accessible climbing on generally sound rhyolite, though there are some looser areas.

Towards the left-hand end of the crag is a slender pillar of rock known as Middlefell Buttress which is bounded on the right by Mendes Wall. Several routes take this short steep section of darker rock, the finest of which is Mendes itself. Graded VS, it is the most fallen from route in the valley and probably deserves an upgrade to Hard VS. Whilst climbing on Raven, I have seen three falls from the same place on the route, fortunately only one of which caused any sort of serious injury, breaking the ankle of a climber who fell a little too far and caught his foot on a ledge. The climb has a certain feel to it, partly due to its steepness, partly due to the nature of the rock which is a little brittle in parts, and perhaps also due to its name. I have always felt a little uneasy climbing the route, and the events of a couple of years ago have only reinforced this.

I was taking a small family group of Americans for some navigational skills training on Loughrigg when the call-out happened. Though I would not normally leave my clients stranded on a mountainside, in view of the fact that we were almost back to the road, and that this was an emergency, I bade them farewell, ran down to the car and drove straight to the Old Dungeon Ghyll, where the reports were that a climber had fallen from Middlefell Buttress. Several rescuers were ahead of me, including Sarah Hollis, an ex-team member and first-class doctor who was visiting the area. I joined the file of people trudging up the pitched stone path to the crag and soon realised that the injured party lay not beneath Middlefell, but directly under Mendes. Two climbers had been injured, one in only a relatively minor way, so we concentrated on the one who lay on the steep, bracken-clad slope. He couldn't have picked a worse place to come to rest if he had tried. The ground was extremely steep, the earth was covered with a thick layer of old, decaying bracken stems and the resulting morass was exceedingly 'slape' – local dialect for slippery.

Sarah had examined the casualty as best she could, and it was clear that his back injuries were very painful and potentially very serious. Nothing could be done until he was anchored securely to prevent any possibility of him falling further down the slope and causing further injury. Fortunately, there was a huge block detached from the main face above and to the side of his position. This was ideal as it meant that a line could be secured without having to climb directly above him, which always poses potential dangers of stonefall or slippage of some sort. Once a line had been secured, we had to get him into a back splint and onto a stretcher.

This sounds easy enough, but on terrain such as that, it proved to be an extremely delicate operation which required great patience and skill. Under Sarah's expert supervision, we gingerly manoeuvred him into a position in which the back splint could be eased beneath him with minimum disturbance. We were all well aware of the potential consequences of a sudden movement or slip, and there were some tense moments until this was accomplished.

The back splint is a curved, semi-stiff plastic corset, which is designed to hug around the neck, shoulders, ribs and waist, and which fastens across the front with wide webbing straps which effectively immobilise the upper body. Once attached to this, the casualty is certainly in a better position to be moved, though it is by no means a guarantee that further injury is not possible.

A fallen climber is particularly susceptible to back injuries, either from the general shock of the impact, or more particularly if he lands on his feet, when a compression fracture can occur, as the shock of landing is transferred from the feet, up through the legs and into the spinal column. As it compresses, it can trap the spinal chord, or individual vertebrae can fracture or dislocate, leaving the chord bent or trapped and in danger of sustaining further damage, which could, of course, be permanent. With all this in mind, dealing with any back injury is a delicate affair and I for one was glad when he was securely strapped to the stretcher, apparently in no worse condition than when we found him.

Whilst all this had been taking place, a helicopter had arrived on the scene, and as the winchman came down, rescuers not involved in the final evacuation scurried out of the way. (Ever since the Sea King helicopter accident in Eskdale, when a rotor touched the rock face and sheared off, people seem only too happy to move well back out of the way whenever a crag winching is taking place!) I scrambled up to hide behind the pinnacle which the belay rope had been attached to, and if there was ever a time I wished I had a camera, this was it, for I was right up at helicopter level, with the rotors flashing round not twenty metres away. The pilot edged the helicopter closer and closer to the crag until he was directly above the casualty and winchman, who clipped the winchwire to the stretcher slings before raising his hand to signal that they were prepared for the ride up. As the wire retracted into its winch, the pilot eased the craft slowly away from the crag, taking them steadily away from the main danger zone and towards the hope offered by hospitalisation and medical help.

We cleared the area of our kit and headed down the path to the Old Dungeon Ghyll, where we had the opportunity of talking to the other climber involved, who had been leading. Apparently, some twenty or so feet up the first pitch, the leader had found the going a bit tough, and decided to retreat. He had climbed down as far as his last running belay placement, and slipped, taking what appeared to be a very short fall onto it. At this point, something failed and he fell off the crag, ten or fifteen feet onto the steep ground below, tumbling past his second man, who was ripped from his stance, ending up in the difficult position in which we found him. A final twist to the tale came when the climber produced a karabiner which had been used as part of the extension system off his runner. The gate had been snapped in half, and dangled open, inviting any number of explanations – some sort of obscure leverage, a bang onto the rock face? No one will ever know, but the curse of Mendes had struck again. The injured climber recovered, but not sufficiently to ever climb again.

Raven Crag attracts so many climbers that accidents such as the Mendes incident are almost inevitable, and one which occurred recently was one of the most dramatic. I was running the second day of a climbing course, on which the students had progressed well enough to tackle Middlefell Buttress, one of the finest beginner's multi-pitch climbs in the Lakes. The day was as good as you can get anywhere, azure skies, hot sunshine and a cooling breeze bringing fresh clean air with stunning visibility. Our group was mixed in every sense. Graham and Pete were outgoing Geordies with a sharp sense of humour and an incredible capacity for drinking beer, whilst at the other end of the spectrum were Anne and Julie, both shy and a little nervous, but determined to get to grips with rock climbing, despite their natural aversion to standing on anything higher than a table top.

We had climbed three pitches at a lazy pace, practising ropework and belaying skills, trying layback holds, mantelshelf moves and chimneying techniques, when we congregated on a spacious ledge (spacious for a rock climb anyway) for a final debriefing before lunch. A shout alerted us initially, and in the instant we turned to source the noise, we simultaneously heard and saw a huge fall take place from the central part of the main crag, which was 200 feet or so to our right. It all happened with such bewildering speed that it took a few seconds for the reality of what had occurred to sink in. We had seen the climber complete what must have been a forty- or fifty-foot fall, banging hard onto a ledge on the way down and coming to rest, still, in the branches of a stout oak which sprouted from the first pitch of Holly Tree Traverse.

There was a strange momentary silence before various exclamations and somewhat optimistic shouts of 'Are you all right?' brought everyone back to their senses. My fellow instructor on the day was Dave Willis, a professional instructor and specialist outdoor photographer. After restraining his natural instinct for that front page scoop photo opportunity, Dave made certain that everyone in our group was secure, and we both scrambled down the gully with indecent alacrity, probably fortunate not to have twisted an ankle or knocked rocks on each other in the process. Dave continued his sprint down to the Old Dungeon Ghyll to call the team out and to grab the pacman sac from the team's advance base, whilst I dashed across to the accident scene. The logic behind this was simply that Dave was likely to be faster than I down to the Old Dungeon and back, while I had more experience of casualty care in these situations. Having said this, no amount of experience can really prepare you for such an unexpected scenario, and I was not looking forward to my rendezvous with the fallen climber in the branches of the gnarly old oak.

There are so many things to think about. What do you do if . . . he's unconscious, he's not breathing, he's got bad head injuries . . .

The questions raced through my mind, but few answers clicked into place. The responsibility of being first on the scene is daunting in cases such as this where the potential injuries might require instant decision-making which could have life or death consequences. The problem is that although there are many rescues, there are only a limited number of times on which any one individual is likely to be first on the scene, and only a small number of these incidents are likely to require the sort of primary first aid care which can give us the required experience. In spite of advanced first aid training, specialised equipment and simulated scenarios, the vast majority of rescuers are still unprepared by virtue of lack of practice to deal confidently with serious injury or medical conditions.

I climbed solo up the V-shaped groove beneath the tree in which the climber lay, and eased myself through the branches until I was level with him. Above me, his second turned to reveal a familiar face. Helen was a friend who was well-known and liked around Ambleside, a happy and carefree lass who had been a little unlucky to have been on the receiving end of her leader's impressive 'lob', as some climbers would call a fall. She had severe rope burns on her hands after trying to arrest the falling climber through her belay plate, but was otherwise uninjured. After making all the necessary reassuring noises, and ensuring that no climbers above us could make things worse by dislodging loose rock, I clipped onto a sling wrapped round a branch above the climber and started to examine him.

He was conscious. That was good, as he could tell me where it hurt, thus reducing the chances of making an incorrect diagnosis. His name was Tom and, miraculously, he appeared to be in quite good shape – that is considering he had fallen thirty feet or so onto a rock ledge, bounched off this and landed after another thirty feet in the solid branches of a tree. Injuries apart, it dawned on me that we had quite a major problem with Tom as he was jammed between the multi-stemmed tree trunk and the rock face, curled around in a most awkward posture and with virtually no room for manoeuvre whatsoever. The space available was far too small to accommodate even one half of the team's stretcher, and administering any first aid was clearly going to be difficult.

I proceeded with my examination, noticing with surprise how quickly Dave had returned with the first aid kit. I and most others would have still been struggling up the path below. Tom had some head injuries, but they didn't look too serious and his consciousness levels were essentially normal. Hardly surprisingly, his legs had been knocked about a bit, and looking at the deformities present, I suspected that there was at least one fracture. He had back pain, which concerned me, and a shoulder injury which was obviously painful. As I examined him we chatted about the accident, and it transpired that some of the running belays which he had placed had come out after the fall, resulting in him taking a much longer 'whipper' (another name for a fall), than would normally have been expected.

The rest of the team were now arriving with extra equipment, ropes and radios, but most of them could do little to help as the space available was so restricted. I was fortunate in then receiving assistance from two of the team's more experienced members. Martin came down to join me on the ledge, as confident and reassuring as usual, and Mike Withers appeared above us with instructions to arrange anchor points and ropes for the eventual stretcher lower. With some relief, Martin's casualty assessment confirmed my diagnosis – no apparent major injuries, but possible back problems and serious difficulties regarding the evacuation from the ledge. Tom had so many minor injuries that it took some time to bandage and tape him up, each dressing presenting us with problems which would have been better given to a contortionist, so tight was the space in which we had to work. Yet all this paled into insignificance with the next problem, which was how to slide the back splint into place without the aid of a tree surgeon.

Martin and I somehow manoeuvred ourselves into positions in which we could lift Tom, though balancing between the tree's branches and the rock face was precarious in the extreme, and with a combination of brute strength, cunning, a little skill and a lot of luck, we eventually had him in the splint. So far, so good. The next problem we faced was that the space available to us was far too narrow to even contemplate using the standard Bell stretcher, and as lowering Tom was the only option available, he had to be strapped to something secure to avoid the high probability of further injury being caused. The answer came with the helicopter, which carries a Neil Robertson stretcher, commonly used in confined situations such as mines and caves. It's a narrow device, with a hard base and flexible side pieces which wrap around the casualty, keeping it as slim as possible. This has one significant disadvantage in lowering on cliffs, as the casualty does not benefit from the protection which the wider Bell stretcher provides, so cautious handling is essential.

We decided that we would have to slide the stretcher beneath Tom from behind, which was always going to be a Herculean task as Tom was no lightweight and Martin and I had precious little in the way of secure ground to stand on and lift. An individual of something less than Herculean proportions was required to squeeze down behind the tree and slide the stretcher forwards as Martin and I lifted Tom up. It was Mike Withers, I think, a little powerhouse who fitted the bill perfectly, who eased the stretcher into position as we heaved, as gently as it is possible to heave, until the stretcher was exactly beneath Tom. Other team members had secured ropes above us for lowering, and it was clear that the stretcher would have to be guided down by one of us to avoid it snagging and banging on the rock face. This job has the rather demeaning title of 'barrow boy', after the way in which the rescuer involved appears to be wheeling the stretcher, barrow-like, down the rock face. It's very similar to pushing a wheelbarrow, with one or two subtle differences, such as the fact that there are no wheels, that there is an injured body aboard and that it takes place on a vertiginous rock face. Modern jargon could surely come up with an improved name – 'stretcher management co-ordinator' perhaps, or 'rock face casualty evacuation officer'.

Whatever the title, it didn't alter the fact that this was the trickiest part of the rescue, and it had been tricky enough already. As I was closest to the edge, I was elected for the job, and clipped onto a rope which snaked down through the tree like a lazy underfed python. Blindly trusting whoever was holding the rope, I leaned back over the drop and, assisted most capably by Martin, Tom was gradually released from the confines of his arboreal captor and shifted laterally in as calm and unruffled a manner as was possible in the circumstances. We were suddenly leaning over the wide groove beneath us, which looked rather like an open book tilted up at 80 degrees. Co-ordination was of the essence at this point, and the lowering had to be just at the right speed so that I could fend the stretcher away from the rock to avoid jarring or snagging. Due to the shape of the rock face, this meant opening my legs as wide as possible so that one touched each retaining wall of the groove, in a bridging position, whilst I pulled Tom away from the crag so that he hung in space. It was not easy, and my nerves were as taut as the ropes. The situation was not helped by the distance between the stretcher and the lowering points and twice, as the stretcher and I suddenly dropped a short distance, a wide range of graphic expletives left no doubt as to my dissatisfaction. I felt a little guilty afterwards at getting so ratty, as the lowerers were doing their best to ensure a smooth passage in what were onerous conditions. (Sorry lads.) Thirty or so feet later we arrived on terra firma to receiving arms which held Tom clear of the rock and lowered him gently to the ground. All that was left was for the helicopter to perform a dramatic but straightforward winch and Tom was quickly transported to hospital.

He sent me a postcard shortly afterwards and I was really delighted to find that he had suffered only relatively minor injuries, and had no back problems. He was certainly fortunate in this respect, but perhaps unfortunate to be the subject of a major feature in the *Sun* newspaper which declared that his life had been saved by the tree, which cushioned the blow.

One of the most bizarre call-outs on Raven Crag occurred one evening at about throwing out time. Customers at the Old Dungeon Ghyll reported seeing flashing lights and hearing shouts – nothing unusual perhaps after several pints of Old Peculiar, in fact these would probably be the least of your worries. But the reports were from a variety of folk, some of whom were undoubtedly sober. For once, I arrived at the Old Dungeon before everyone else and, armed with a pacman sac and a rope, I set off for the crag. The lights had been seen at the top of Middlefell Buttress, so I aimed for Middlefell Gully, a steep gash on the left of the buttress which is notorious for its loose rock, but which is the normal descent from the route and also the easiest way of getting to the top. In front of me was a local climber and musician, Mick Mead, who had no doubt had a wonderful guitar-playing, beer-swilling, chorus-singing evening in the Old Dungeon before very nobly wandering up the fellside to see if he could help. He had, in fact, made contact with the persons responsible for the flashing lights and was able to shout down to me that they were somewhere above him. It was a typically unselfish and well-meaning effort to help which is so often found within the climbing community, where everyone appreciates the fact that accidents can happen to anyone at any time.

The scramble up the gully starts off as a simple scree slope with a few loose boulders, but it soon steepens into a final amphitheatre of cliffs and fault lines, one of which leads increasingly steeply out to a narrow grassy neck of fellside which splits the main section of Middlefell Buttress from the final pitch, which some people know as the Curtain Wall (so called because it's curtains if you fall off it!). Before arriving on the ledge, I made contact with the group and it was clear that they were all OK, but extremely stuck. At that stage I assumed that they had failed to finish the climb in the light, and been overtaken by a darkness so black that they were unable to move from their location. As I scrambled onto the ledge to join them, I realised that the scenario I had imagined was not going to hold up.

There were four of them, one 'leader' who was probably in his thirties, plus three teenagers who looked ready for a night out joy-riding in Liverpool (which ironically was where they were from). They proceeded to inundate me with a barrage of high-speed Scouse explanations as to why they were where they were, none of which made much sense because I couldn't understand their accents. However, after urging them to slow down and compose themselves, it transpired that they had arrived on the ledge after trying to find a path down from their evening walk. The direction in which they assured me they had come from was the top pitch of the climb, Curtain Wall, and there was no way they could possibly have descended that. Or if they had, they wouldn't have spent the last couple of hours stuck on such relatively easy terrain. Further questioning revealed little new information and they were ada-mant that they had not ascended to the ledge from the gully, which would be the only realistic way there for a non-climber. I decided that they were either lying, severely mistaken or blessed with the sort of levitational properties which Tibetan monks could only dream about.

Other team members arrived with ropes, harnesses, helmets and the hand-held spotlights which run from a compact car-type battery carried in a rucsac. These lights really can illuminate whole sections of the crag, and they are invaluable on any rescue of this type. Malcolm Grindrodd, who is the 'Captain Searchdog' of the team, arrived on the ledge and helped gear the lads up for their descent. Malcolm possesses a slow Lancastrian drawl which con-ceals a sometimes wicked sense of humour, and as a long-standing deputy team leader and leading light in the search dog world, he has dedicated his life to rescue work in the most genuine and selfless way. We had decided simply to truss the lads up in harnesses, strap a helmet on each of them and lower them a hundred feet down the gully to the easy scree slopes below.

One of the oldest rowan trees I have ever seen overhangs the cliff edge at this point, its roots both spreading through the shallow turf and creeping deep within every open seam the rock presents, until they bulge out, seemingly gripping the edges of the cracks like a hungry octopus to increase their precarious hold on life. We placed a sling around the tree to act as an anchor point and, as Malcolm belayed the boys from the ledge, they initially had to scramble a short way down until beneath the tree. Then I clipped the rope to them and gave them a brief rundown on what to expect: 'Lean back, feet apart, don't try and climb down, just let yourself be lowered.' Seconds later, the first youth was on his way, cast in a surreal spotlight along with the eerie shadows which flinched and stuttered against the huge shield of rock which fringes the gully. His lower was quick, bordering on merciless – it was 2 am after all. The next youth went down with little difficulty and we soon found that the third youth positively enjoyed the experience. The rescuers in the gully bed, who had taken each of the stranded party into their care at the end of the lower, reported that this individual had asked if he could have another go – and meant it. I understand he was sent on his way down the remainder of the gully with the verbal equivalent of a thick ear!

9

SEARCH

If you are someone like me, used to roving the local countryside hunting for folk who should be where you've been told they are, but often aren't, it comes as a bit of a surprise when you encounter something which shouldn't be where you come across it, but very manifestly is.

Following a simple call-out early one fair summer's evening to Stickle Ghyll to attend to a sprained ankle, most team members retired to the pub for a quick pint, courtesy of the Stickle Barn Tavern before returning to base or home. Who was I to differ, though on the way back down the valley, I had cause to ponder on the strength of the local brew, for a couple of hundred yards or so down the 'old road' which runs directly from near Harry Place Farm to the New Dungeon Ghyll I spotted a telephone box. So what, you might ask? Well, for starters not only was there no telephone box there that morning, but there never had been. It's also not exactly a roadside position. Most passers-by would never have even noticed it. It had to be worth further investigation. We parked up and casually ambled down towards the box which was warmly illuminated, in contrast to the gloom of dusk. It contained no telephone and appeared to be completely and utterly devoid of any use whatsoever. An elaborate hoax perhaps, or maybe the BT engineers had been given the wrong grid reference. As we pondered on these and ever more ridiculous possibilities, a couple of rotund characters rocked their way down the track towards us.

'Evening,' I casually enquired. 'Is this yours then?' As if most passers-by leave stray phone boxes on remote bridlepaths.

They confessed to being the perpetrators of this bizarre manifestation, and turned out to be a pair of slick ad-men, bent on getting that all important message across to the unsuspecting public. Which all important message you may ask? It's obvious – that whenever and wherever you need a call box, there is always one close to hand! A photographer had been lurking on the fellsides waiting for the right moment to shoot pictures of the illuminated red booth, and the resulting shot would provide a shining example of how thoughtfully BT place their public payphones. Pity they forgot to put a telephone in it. I thought it was all a bit of a cheek anyway, considering that BT have consistently refused to place a call box at the head of Langdale where there is a genuine need for one.

Locating illuminated telephone boxes is of course considerably easier than locating missing persons on the fells, though you have a considerably greater chance of being found swiftly these days than in the first part of the century, when rescue teams did not exist and very few people knew the mountains well enough to search them anywhere near thoroughly, a fact exemplified by an early rescue operation which took place amongst the rubble-strewn fells of the Scafell Massif at the head of Wasdale in 1921. This beautiful mountain and its neighbouring peaks are deceptively sized. One famous occasion in Victorian times saw an Alpine guide trying to estimate the point at which their party should have to bivouac for the night on their ascent of Great Gable. He was somewhat embarrassed when they reached the top two hours later. They are fine mountains which rank with the best in Britain, and they are seen at their most magnificent from one of the many superb viewpoints on the opposite side of Wasdale Head, such as

Kirk Fell. They have always acted as a magnet for walkers and climbers, and they proved to be a dangerously strong one for a man who set out to walk up Scafell that summer. Expected back at 7 pm, he decided, in view of the fair conditions, to continue his walk in the direction of Styhead, but at the col between Scafell Pike and Broad Crag, he became tempted to descend via Piers Gill. The gill was first ascended direct in 1893 by a party of four, possibly providing the ammunition for one of the earlier guidebooks to describe the route as 'Best climbed on a hot day with a large jolly party,' but as every good fellsman or fellswoman knows, gills are dangerous places, and best avoided on descent. After all, water generally takes the easiest line, and the easiest line is often the steepest. Piers Gill is undoubtedly one of the finest of its type, and has been described as one of the most 'solemn and dramatic gullies in the Kingdom'. It cleaves a huge incision up the north-eastern flank of Lingmell, with two right-angled kinks giving it a unique configuration. The walker involved in our incident made a major error of judgement in deciding to descend the left bank of the gill, by far the harder of the two sides, and some way down disaster struck and he slipped down towards the base of the gill, landing on a ledge and fracturing both ankles. Dividing what was left of his sandwich and gingerbread into even more meagre rations, he waited, hoped and shouted. In a modern summer, he would probably have attracted attention very quickly, or a search party or helicopter would have spotted him. But the fells were still relatively lonely then, and gorge scrambling had not even started its heady rise to its present-day levels of popularity. Day after day searchers looked but found no trace of the missing man and any hopes of finding him alive steadily evaporated, as sure as the water in the heatwave of time. Meanwhile in the gill the heatwave probably seemed of little consequence as time ebbed by. Kept alive by a trickle of water which flowed past his ledge, and by a courage and endurance beyond the imagination of most of us, the walker held on.

In a way, it was the heatwave which saved him, for the cascades of Piers Gill dried to a trickle and its opalescent turquoise pools warmed enough to attract a group of climbers intent on climbing the gill whilst it was in such lenient conditions. It was the eighteenth day since his fall, and who could possibly imagine his feelings on finally being discovered by this group. It was a miraculous event, quite unprecedented and still without equal as the most amazing feat of human endurance in the history of Lake District rescue. These days rescue teams would have hoped to find him within a day or two at most.

Searching the fells for missing persons can be a frustrating and at times maddening pursuit. The fact that someone is missing and potentially lost or hurt in the mountains is enough to motivate rescue teams, but so often the information on the casualty's whereabouts is so sketchy and inadequate that it really can be like looking for a needle in a haystack, or perhaps a shepherd's crook on a mountain would be more appropriate. Search dogs can help, and are capable of covering large areas of rough land faster and more efficiently than any human, but there are hidden corners, gullies and crags that remain out of bounds to most of these energetic canine helpers.

The use of search dogs in mountain rescue work has become a very specialised topic, involving highly trained dogs and dedicated handlers who have their own organisation, the Search And Rescue Dog Association (SARDA). Many types of dogs have been used for this purpose in the past – alsatians, setters, labradors for example, but the majority of search dogs now used are border collies or cur dogs (collie cross dogs, often from farms). They have a number of key advantages. They are fast and capable of running huge distances over rough terrain. They have a keen sense of smell and are extremely adaptable. They train well, and can be controlled from some distance away. Perhaps their only major fault is a liking for rounding up or chasing sheep, though this desire has to be curbed completely if they are to be accepted as search dogs.

Both handler and dog have to undergo training and assessment if they are to qualify for membership of SARDA and become a useful team. The assessment is rigorous. The dog must respond to commands instantly and must not even glance at a sheep. It must search steep and rocky fellsides in a logical and thorough manner, and it must find a number of pre-placed hidden casualties. The standards are high, and handler and dog alike need to be trained and prepared for even the most severe conditions.

Many calls for assistance in cases where fell walkers and climbers are overdue never appear on rescue statistics, yet they can create a huge amount of work for team leaders and their assistants, not to mention the local Police. In the vast majority of cases, those involved turn up shortly afterwards, having underestimated the length of their journey or overestimated their fitness levels. In some instances, missing walkers turn up in public houses or similar establishments, blissfully unaware that others may be concerned or even searching for them. Occasionally, they turn up in locations where they did not intend to be found – a lover's house or the wrong tent for example! Bearing all this in mind, I suspect that many rescue team members react with some degree of indifference when a search for an overdue party is activated, though it has to be said that all searches, no matter how apparently trivial, are carried out with the same degree of commitment and tenacity.

One search which started out with a certain degree of vagueness became one of the most noteworthy cases of its type in mountain rescue – that for a French student, Veronique Marre. She was on a solo-walking holiday, though inadequately equipped for some of the district's rough terrain, when she disappeared somewhere between Wasdale Youth Hostel and Grasmere. One of the largest scale searches was launched, and after rescue teams and the RAF had failed to locate any trace of her, the Police used between twenty and thirty men each day in an unfortunately fruitless operation centred on the Wastwater region. The search for Veronique was called off in 1984, months after her disappearance in July 1983, and after even an attempt to find her through the BBC *Crimewatch* programme had failed. She was eventually located two years later, in a remote chasm known as Broken Rib Gully, high above Wastwater, where it appeared she had slipped approximately 300 feet, possibly due to the fact that she was wearing smooth-soled sandals. The searches for Veronique did however lead to another startling discovery, that of a woman's body, weighted down in England's deepest lake. What followed hit the headlines as the 'Lady in the Lake' case, and the lady's husband, pilot Peter Hogg, was later jailed for manslaughter after it was revealed that he dumped the body into Wastwater from a light aircraft.

Another form of search which has become increasingly commonplace is that which takes place following the sighting of flashing lights, or after shouts for help have been heard. Small groups of rescuers would often be despatched into the major valleys, such as Langdale, to check on the latest sightings, which might range from groups messing about with torches to walkers descending in the dark whose movement caused their head torches to bob about and appear to flash. On one occasion, a camera flash was successfully used to attract attention. The vast majority of flashing light incidents are false alarms, but the fact that six flashes of a light constitutes the internationally recognised distress signal gives each sighting a definite reason for investigation. Shouts for help are more commonly heard than made. The critical noises are often derived from the local sheep-farming industry. Many a bleating sheep heard on a day when the winds distort could easily be mistaken for a desperate cry for assistance by the uninitiated, and every shepherd's dog has either a name or a command which, from a distance, sounds just like 'Help!' Listen the next time you're out! On more than one occasion we have searched an area from which cries for help were supposed to have been heard to find nothing at all, but to disover later that sheep gathering had been taking place in the area.

Though many searches are based on unreliable information, one local search I can recall required little skill and resolve on our part, such was the accuracy of the given location for the missing persons. A local pub landlord and his brother were out celebrating – not in a Kendal or Barrow nightclub, or even on an Ambleside pub crawl, but on a local felltop. Determined to celebrate in style by drinking a bottle of fine whisky atop the rocky knolls of Side Pike, one suspects they must have been already somewhat under the influence before departing for their summit bid.

The pair had been gone for some considerable time before assistance was summoned in the early hours, and the ensuing search was as easy as any. One of the two was found giggling as he grappled with a fence on the descent from Side Pike to the Blea Tarn road, seemingly oblivious to the low temperatures and barbed wire. His drinking partner was found sprawled unconscious on the summit with an empty bottle of whisky abandoned at this side. There has to be a lesson here somewhere – though if there is, it was not one heeded by another group of revellers some years later!

Side Pike overlooks the public bar of the Old Dungeon Ghyll and though a severely altitude challenged peak, even by Langdale standards, its shapely summit cone and easy access tempt many to discuss an intended ascent over a few pints of Old Peculiar. This is no recipe for success, though, and this is one case in which words generally speak louder than actions. One group of young men did take things further than the bar, but unfortunately did not await the onset of the following dawn, electing instead for a drunken night-time clamber – all part of the fun arranged for the intended husband on his stag night. We'll never know the exact course of events between 'throwing out time' and the call-out, which I think was about 3 am, but I can recall being extremely confused by a call to a climbing accident on Side Pike at that hour. So confused in fact that it took another sympathetic, though highly amused team member to tell me that I was not wearing any trousers when I turned up to help.

Side Pike has a short but steep crag falling from the eastern side of its summit, varying between 70 and 120 feet in height. Our drunken lads had made it to the summit, but in attempting to descend, the best man had fallen over the edge of the cliff, landing about a hundred feet below on rough ground. Though his injuries were serious enough, with fractured ankles, lacerations, severe bruising and a head injury, our doctor was convinced that only his relaxed state, induced by intoxication, had saved him from more serious injury. Some team members had to be restrained from going back to the Old Dungeon Ghyll for a few pints 'just in case'. I was told that the best man made his appearance some time later at the wedding day on crutches, but gave one of the most entertaining and unusual wedding speeches ever!

The major village of Langdale, Chapel Stile, (apologies to those who live in Elterwater) is as close to an archetypal Lakeland village as you can get. Its church is set below steep fellsides whose slopes glow golden brown in the autumn as the bracken dies off. Dozens of small slaty outcrops of rock pepper the same hillsides, mirroring the gentle grey hues and even the architecture of the church and nearby cottages. The village school still thrives and in the Langdale Co-operative we have a shop which supplies everything from shoelaces to salami. Noise from the local quarry can be substantial, but is never intrusive. Blasting explosions and the rumbling of waste rock as it is dumped on the spoil heaps are little competition for the low-flying aircraft which regularly skim perilously close to the fellsides.

There are other, more up to date, factors which typify the modern Lakeland village. A Timeshare on the outskirts of Chapel Stile is now larger than the village itself. Though the concept of a Time-share in Langdale outraged many people at the time of its inception, I view it as a generally good thing. It must reduce the seemingly insatiable demand for holiday homes significantly, and it provides a considerable amount of employment for locals. It also has an excellent firework display every November! Despite the abundance of holiday accommodation at the Timeshare, around sixty per cent of houses in the village are second homes, many retired people have moved into the area and prices carry a hefty Langdale weighting. On busy days, traffic crawls relentlessly back and forth and trying to get a quiet pint at the local pub is a complete waste of time. To survive, it seems that popular Lakeland villages must put up with or even encourage this intrusion, with little room for compromise.

In Chapel Stile, nothing is more local than the Co-op. Managed and staffed by real locals, the shop stocks an amazing variety of goods and a trip upstairs is recommended to anyone wanting to relive the 1960s. It would make a fine set for a series such as *Heartbeat*. Whilst a warm welcome is extended to anyone who has lived locally for the past ten years or more, others have reported difficulty in getting a welcome any warmer than the December ice covering Langdale Beck. In fairness though, it's great to see a truly local shop thriving in spite of the competition from centralised superstore shopping.

The first shop-worker to arrive at the very same Co-op one fine summer's morning a few years ago found a note pinned to the door. A secret love letter for the manager perhaps, or a pre-placed order for two loaves and a pint of milk? In fact the note was considerably stranger than the event. Its scrawled handwriting read something like this: 'There is a man lying injured in Langdale I have gone to Scotland on a motorbike.' Not much to go on really. Langdale is a big valley and the M6 no doubt carried many motorcycles en route to Scotland. The note was duly handed to the Police, who passed it to our team leader, Stewart Hulse, as soon as they realised that it might possibly involve rescue, thus relieving them of a bit of work. Everyone decided, quite correctly, that nothing could possibly be done.

I was at home that morning, catching up on some paperwork and enjoying the sunshine of High Close, when the familiar bleeping startled me into something approaching life. I drove out onto the road, without hitting our gates for a change, and waited at the top of Red Bank – a perfect high-level reception point – for the details of the incident to be transmitted over the radio. 'All Langdale Mobiles from Ambleside base, All Langdale Mobiles from Ambleside base. Call-out. Call-out. Man with back injuries above Thrang Quarries at Chapel Stile.' Only a few minutes away, I might even get there first for a change! I drove down to Chapel Stile safely, but at speeds which make the tourists shudder, and parked by the track which leads up to the quarries at the rear of the village, carefully abandoning the car directly in front of one of the plethora of No Parking signs which adorn the holiday homes hereabouts. I chatted to the informants, a family group, and got a rough position for the casualty. I was soon joined by Graham Hartley, former vicar of Langdale and one of the most gentle men I have ever met. Mild-mannered and understanding, Graham is a team member in every sense of the expression, and deserves more than his reputation for being the appropriate man to call on where fatalities are involved, though he undoubtedly had his uses in this respect! He later did Gill and me the honour of performing our marriage service, and we could not have picked a finer person. Graham turns out to have had a somewhat adventurous past, and he is especially proud of an old pair of wooden Nordic skis which he keeps in his garage, and some photos from a wild and snowy Norway. Some years before he had skied along the tracks in Langdale and hit the headlines as the skiing vicar, visiting his snowbound parishioners.

A few minutes of hard breathing brought us to the casualty. He lay sprawled across a rough track of scree, on which it was easy at first glance to see how a trip or slip could cause an unpleasant accident. According to his stumbling narrative, he had fallen the previous evening and had lain out all night on this rough patch of loose boulders. I checked him carefully and, though I could find no obvious areas for concern by feel, touching his lower back and thigh brought a terrifying yowl of pain and a contorted expression which made us wince, never mind him. His pain seemed so extreme that we decided to wait for further equipment and a painkilling drug before attempting to immobolise him and start an evacuation. In the meantime, we supported him from below to prevent him slipping any further down the scree and padded his back and head to give him some basic comfort. It's always difficult to talk to someone in extreme pain, but we did our best to make casual conversation and reassure him that the stretcher was on its way and that he would soon be down in the valley. Beyond this, we tried to find out a little more about him personally, and the circumstances behind his fall. Though he was on steep ground, it would have been quite difficult to fall and sustain the sort of injuries he appeared to have without being very careless or clumsy. Having said this, many years of walking in the mountains has led me to believe that there may be more people in this category than one might first imagine. So, there we had it, an apparently careless or clumsy walker, very unlucky, probably with a lower back injury.

After a few minutes of dwindling conversation I noticed two cartons of milk on the path to one side. 'Whose are these?' I enquired casually. 'Mine,' replied our casualty. 'Someone left them for me when they passed me this morning.' Having thought about this for a moment or two, it struck me as a little odd that someone would set out on their morning's walk, come across an injured man who had been out all night, leave him a couple of pints of milk and continue their stroll. Apart from anything else, what were they doing with two spare cartons of milk? Something was not quite right.

The rest of that morning's contingent of rescuers arrived shortly after that. The personnel who turn out on rescues varies quite considerably according to the time of day, and as this was mid-morning, we were overloaded with those who had retired or who were self-employed, and in a position to respond without causing their employers to foam at the mouth too much. I think it was Maureen who gave the injection, a sharp jab of Cyclomorph in the bum which would soon relieve the casualty of such grimace-creating pain. We immobilised him with a back splint and lifted him gently onto the stretcher. By now, he had become quite garrulous, though what he had to say was wandering and some-what bizarre. The carry down was steep, but mercifully short and in fifteen minutes or so, we had him safely down at the ambulance which had blocked yet another holiday home's parking place in the village. Jim, as we shall call our casualty, then proceeded to stun the lot of us by requesting that we go to his rucsac and locate Billy. Billy turned out to be his teddy. Pints of milk, teddies . . . It was all getting a bit much. Further investigations led to the discovery in the rucsac of a cutting from a Carlisle newspaper. It concerned a fire at a house in Carlisle, and the actions of a 'local hero' who had alerted the authorities. The local hero was in fact our casualty, who by now had recovered considerably and was feeling little pain at all. We all wondered about this mysterious incident. Who was he, how badly was he injured, what was the truth? Another clue came when he arrived at the hospital and was seen sitting up and talking eagerly to the nurses, this when he had appeared to be in excruciating pain not long before.

In fact, there was nothing wrong with Jim at all and his story was as fascinating as it was sad. Jim had mental problems and until recently he had lived, by all accounts quite happily, in a home. Government policy at the time had been to try to get people in homes rehabilitated into the community, in this case, seemingly without regard to whether the person could cope with such a move. His personal cry for help had been to instigate a mountain rescue incident and, despite the inconvenience that this caused, I don't think anyone in the team bore any ill-feeling towards Jim. It was he who had left the illiterate note at the Co-op and it was he of course who had taken the milk with him. I'll give him one thing, though, he was a bloody good actor!

The story does not end there. A couple of months later there was another call-out in the Chapel Stile area, this time attended by a predominantly different set of team members. A man had fallen and sustained obviously painful though hard to define injuries. It was Jim again, but this time, unrecognised, and he seemed to be in so much pain that the rescuers felt he needed a hefty injection of morphine, sending him on a free trip! It was not until he was freely hallucinating that someone eventually recognised him, thus giving us a somewhat embarrassed Dave Thompson, for that lively

Geordie who worked for the National Trust as a warden had been on the first Jim rescue, but had failed to recognise him. Someone later described it as a self-inflicted training excercise. By this time, Jim's behaviour was giving us some concern. Every time the team's resources are deployed on an unnecessary call-out such as this, those same resources are not available for any other genuine incidents. Hoax call-outs are thankfully few and far between, and we hoped that Jim would begin to get the message.

The following year, an incident was reported in the upper reaches of Stickle Ghyll. A man was said to have fallen on rocks close to the beck and broken a leg. There was no indication whatsoever that this was anything other than a genuine call-out, and the team assembled outside the Stickle Barn at the foot of the ghyll. This area is a notorious accident black spot, attracting more visitors than any other path in the Lake District. Not only are there more visitors, but a greater percentage of them are ill-prepared for the fells. Many years ago, the paths here were no more than grassy trods along the side of the stream, but the boom in fell walking led to rapid erosion, the steepness of the terrain, frosts and the heavy rainfall increasing the damage created by walkers' boots. The National Trust began an improvement scheme here in the early 1980s and the dramatic improvements which have taken place over the years have been a double-edged sword, improving the appearance of the ghyllside by reducing the erosion, but at the same time encouraging more and more walkers to venture higher than they might otherwise have done. Not only do they explore further into the fells than before, but as the path is constructed and easy to walk on uphill, those with grossly inadequate gear (in particular bad footwear), find no 'natural' block to their progress, save one section just before the levelling to Stickle Tarn. If you care to name a type of footwear, I can guarantee to have seen it on the Stickle Ghyll path! Red high heels, slick town shoes, nailed boots, stilettos, patent knee-length boots, slippers ... even walking boots sometimes! Bearing all this in mind, it came as no surprise that an incident of the type reported had taken place.

157

Martin Scrowston and Sarah Hollis were the first to locate the casualty. They were so often first on the scene, one had to wonder if they had anything else to do, though, to be fair, they were enviably quick on the hills. Both of them fortunately recognised Jim as soon as they saw him and relayed a message back to the rest of the team to inform that there was no need to hurry. No stretchers this time, no morphine (though we wondered if that was what he had come back for!), just a stern word and an uncompromising invitation to walk down himself, unassisted. It was the last in the trilogy of Jim rescues and, despite his personal problems, everyone fervently hoped that he had got the message at last. To date, and to my knowledge, there have been no more call-outs involving Jim, so until the next time we hear of someone finding an injured man, leaving a note on the Co-op door and heading off to Scotland by motorcycle, we'll hope his rescue addiction has been cured.

10

SEA KINGS
IN STEEP PLACES

The first time I ever saw a helicopter involved in a mountain rescue incident was in Cwm Idwal, above the Ogwen valley. I was climbing with another member of the Lake District Ranger Service, Roy Harding, and we had started the day with the famous classic, Grooved Arête, on the East side of Tryfan. Climbing alpine-style with rucsacs and boots, we found the polished crux on the so-called Knight's Move (one move up and three across) pleasantly challenging and the remainder of the climb just flowed by, so in high spirits we sprinted to the summit to make the much photographed step from Adam to Eve. (These are the two boulders, often mistaken for people, for readers who may be wondering.)

Roy was in a blisteringly good mood. Not well known as a garrulous conversationalist, Roy's speech often consisted of a series of short grunts, each of a slightly different pitch, and delivered at a range of speeds and volumes which had specific meanings. It was a bit like simplified morse code really. On this day however, such was the geniality of the occasion that Roy spoke almost constantly on the descent from Tryfan into Cwm Idwal, and in this mood he is one of the most interesting people you could wish to spend a day on the hills with, enthusiastic and well-versed in mountain ecology, humorous and with a splendid repertoire of assorted tales. So it was in fine fettle that we set our aim for the massive grey sweep of Idwal Slabs, a popular training ground for beginners and with some very high quality slab routes in the easy to middle grades. We were wanting to climb Tennis Shoe, a soaring rib on the edge of the slabs which had some long run outs and a precarious top section, but our plans were abruptly and shockingly halted when we arrived at the foot of the slabs.

A climber lay huddled, foetus-like amongst the earth and boulders. Blood oozed from a number of head wounds and even at first glance it was clear that he was in a serious condition. The next fifteen minutes or so were a real eye-opener for me, as Roy took charge of the whole situation. An ex-policeman and rescuer of vast experience, his actions were positive, structured and organised with the skill and attention to detail that can only be acquired through both theoretical knowledge and years of practice in dealing with such situations. He made a casualty assessment, carried out what first aid was possible, checked that assistance had been sent for and proceeded to ensure that everything was prepared for a helicopter evacuation. All loose equipment and clothing was secured in rucsacs or under rocks, and the area was cleared of other climbers and walkers ready for the helicopter, which arrived faster than I had imagined possible. It circled the cwm a couple of times, checking winds and assessing the accident site. As it edged towards the foot of the slabs to lower the winchman I felt the down draught from the rotors for the first time. Coupled with the deafening noise from both rotors and engine, it made communication virtually impossible and attaining any position other than a solid crouch was unthinkable.

As suddenly as it came, the noise and wind retreated, leaving the winchman to assess the situation and arrange the evacuation. We carefully lifted the injured man onto a stretcher, wincing ourselves at the pain he must have felt and strapped him securely on. Then, the noise and wind returned as the helicopter settled into a steady hover above us, its slender winchwire snaking down to touch the ground a few metres from the stretcher. It seemed like a long time until all was ready. The stretcher was clipped to the wire, the winchman too, and with a final raise of his arm to signal all was well to the remainder of his crew, the wire tautened and the noise and wind increased to a deafening and boisterous climax as the pilot applied full power and slowly ascended above Llyn Idwal. Silence returned quickly. Only a gentle breeze drifted across the grass and but for the splatter of dark red on the brown earth, it was as if nothing had happened at all.

Slowly, those present started talking again, a little lighthearted-ness fraudulently elevated the atmosphere and there was even talk of climbing. What little we all knew of the incident was shared. No one knew the facts, but the casualty appeared to have fallen the full length of the slabs, about 400 feet. That he had survived the fall was surprising. That he passed away in the helicopter before arriving at hospital was not.

We decided to continue our climb and to place the incident we had happened upon to the back of our minds. It is absolutely vital to do this, and to be able to get on with one's personal climbing without dwelling on what might or could have been. Concentration levels have to be maintained continuously at the highest level and distractions, such as the one we had just witnessed, must be placed in some sort of perspective otherwise you would just never climb again.

Rescues by helicopter have become increasingly commonplace in the late 1980s and 1990s, partly due to the increase in accident frequency and also due to the increasingly good relationship between the RAF helicopter crews and civilian mountain rescue teams. This is great news for the casualties, who can find them-selves whisked from a remote and hostile mountainside to hospital in a matter of minutes, though I have heard a quite unbelievable opinion of disappointment voiced from several rescuers that this has prevented them from being involved in the incident! These are probably the same types who insist on clipping their radiopagers on the outside of their pockets in the pub like so many Sylvester Stallones in *Cliffhanger*.

Helicopters are by any standards expensive, and although most rescue teams would dearly love to have a shiny yellow Sea King sitting in a hangar outside their base, it is just not going to happen. The vast majority of helicopters involved in rescues on British mountains are RAF Sea Kings and Wessex machines, which are stationed at RAF bases such as Boulmer in Northumberland, which serves the Lake District, and Valley on Anglesey which serves much of North Wales. Their principal task is military rescue, but outside this they will assist in virtually any rescue operation on land or sea when they are available and requested. As military incidents are thankfully few and far between just now, much of their work is in fact civilian, and the links between the RAF and civilian rescue teams are better than ever. The increasing use of helicopters in rescue work can be best seen by looking at the statistics. In 1988, just 7.5% of the Langdale team's call-outs benefited from helicopter assistance. In 1989, this figure rose to 14.75%, and in 1990 to 22%. They remain a powerful tool for rescue teams the world over and I can only see their use in this country becoming increasingly established.

Just as a member of the public cannot call out a rescue team without going through the Police, rescue teams cannot call in the services of a helicopter without going through the correct channels. In theory this means the Police liaise through the RAF co-ordination centre at Pitreavie. In practice this is time consuming and in the past has not been without problems, so two other methods which short cut this system may be used. Firstly, the helicopter crews have to put in a certain amount of flying time for practice, and they tend to base much of this activity in the very areas where accidents are most frequent, and often at the peak call-out time during the early part of the afternoon. So when the helicopter arrives in the area, it will try to establish contact with the appropriate rescue base by radio. If the base is manned (unusual except for busier teams such as Langdale/Ambleside which seems to have the benefit of a plethora of members who have little else to do), it will respond and note that there is an available helicopter in the area. In turn, the helicopter will listen in on MR frequency. If a call-out does occur, its assistance can be called upon immediately via MR frequency or via channel 79, the RAF's own rescue frequency to which teams usually have a number of radios tuned. The correct procedures for the involvement of the helicopter can also be carried out, but as a secondary stage, the important thing being to deal with the incident as speedily as possible.

If, however, the helicopter is on the ground at RAF Boulmer, for example, and its assistance is required, some teams may have a hotline direct to the flight crew at the base. Using this, precious minutes can be saved as the craft is ready for take off immediately the official procedures have been followed. Helicopters are only requested from their base when the casualty is sufficiently badly injured to require speedy evacuation. Examples would be a casualty with head injuries, multiple or serious internal injuries or a heart attack, where serious deterioration or loss of life is a possibility. To contrast the standard method of evacuation with that by helicopter, the following example may be illuminating.

Let's say we have a casualty suffering from serious head injuries on the top of Crinkle Crags. Conventionally, the following procedure and approximate times would apply. Firstly, the informant reaches a telephone and calls out the rescue team via the Police. Our clock is now set at 00 00hrs. The police activate the call-out procedure, rescue team members' bleepers bleep and the first person to the base telephones the Police for the information. The first Land Rover leaves the base approximately ten minutes after the call-out starts. Along with other independent vehicles, it arrives at the top of Wrynose Pass twenty to twenty-five minutes later. The fastest team members leave for the casualty location and arrive after another fifty minutes. This puts us at 1hr 20mins elapsed time. First aid is performed and the casualty is prepared for evacuation, whilst the stretcher arrives and is assembled ready for the carry down. 1hr 40mins. The carry back to the top of Wrynose Pass takes another hour, giving us 2hrs 40mins, and the ambulance to the hospital in Kendal requires another forty-five minutes, giving a total elapsed time of 3hrs 25mins. The hospital in Kendal decides that it cannot deal adequately with the nature of the injuries and requests a transfer to Newcastle which has a specialist neurosurgical unit. The transfer takes another 1hr 45mins, giving a total time elapsed since the call out of 5hrs 10mins.

Our second scenario uses the helicopter right from the start. The call-out response time is the same at ten minutes, but at this stage the helicopter has already been requested and it leaves Boulmer ten minutes into the call-out. A doctor plus a few team members await the helicopter's arrival at Ambleside Rugby Club, whilst other team members have to go the traditional route to the casualty on foot, just in case the helicopter fails to arrive or has been diverted to another incident which takes priority. The helicopter arrives in Ambleside in another fifty minutes. It pauses to pick up medical help and continues to the casualty location on Crinkle Crags, where it arrives after another ten minutes. Thus a doctor is on the scene with stretcher and assistants in 1hr 10mins. Allowing twenty minutes for treatment, loading onto the stretcher and winching into the helicopter, we are leaving the accident site in 1hr 30mins. Meanwhile, the team members who are walking up to the casualty site turn round and walk back again. The transfer to Newcastle Hospital takes a further fifty minutes, resulting in a total elapsed time of 2hrs 20mins, almost three hours faster than by normal methods and possibly the difference between life and death. If the helicopter happened to be in the area already, the casualty could be in the same hospital in just over an hour from the alarm being raised. No wonder that a recent report into mountain rescue in the Lake District concluded that the use of a helicopter on a full time basis would be one of the few avenues open to improving the efficiency of an already effective service.

The initial decision of whether to call for helicopter assistance or not is the difficult one. Langdale/Ambleside team leader Stewart

Hulse had no doubts – call for it straight away if there is a chance it could be needed. It can always turn round and go back. For maximum benefit, the helicopter must always be requested as early as possible in the proceedings and, for this reason alone, it becomes paramount that the information provided by the informant be as accurate and as detailed as possible. Most rescuers would suggest that informants always look on the black side of things. If they suspect a sprained ankle, it should be described as a broken ankle, a bad cut on the head ought to be a fractured skull and chest pains a heart attack. This makes a lot of sense, as most people would find an accurate diagnosis difficult to make at the best of times, let alone on a mountainside in a time of crisis.

The advantage of the helicopter can be clearly seen simply in terms of the speed with which a casualty can be delivered to hospital, but there are other factors which are important. Rescue personnel can be airlifted to key positions in the event of a search taking place and the helicopter itself can cover a huge search area. Medical assistance or specialist equipment can be transported to remote areas quickly and the very fact that the helicopter is attending the call-out is a morale booster for everyone. In the Langdale/Ambleside team, not only did it fulfil this purpose, but it also acted as an incentive for team members to get to the casualty site extremely fast. Indeed, it was considered a challenge to get someone there before the helicopter arrived and it was certainly not unusual to hear the familiar voices of the fastest team members, such as Martin Scrowston or Norman Walker, on the radio from the casualty site before the arrival of members in the helicopter.

It has to be said that there are also a few disadvantages about relying on helicopters. They can be called to other higher priority incidents whilst en route to yours, they may suddenly have to disappear to refuel, they can develop mechanical problems and, very occasionally, they crash.

In order that rescue teams can make best use of such an expensive piece of equipment, and in order that they can conform with all the relevant safety issues, appropriate training is essential.

Most teams train with a helicopter crew at least once a year, sometimes twice. The format is almost always the same. A date is arranged, a series of scenarios worked out and on the prescribed morning team members await their turn to be airlifted to pre-defined locations. After all this preparation the helicopter often either arrives late or does not turn up at all! Although this is an all too familiar scenario, when things do go to plan an informative and exciting time is assured.

The first thing we all have to learn about helicopters is basic safety. As you can imagine, they are potentially highly dangerous, with a main and a tail rotor and a scalding hot exhaust, each of which could be lethal. Team members are taught how to approach the parked machine, normally at a 45 degree angle to the pilot on the side to which the main door opens, giving the pilot good visibility and keeping us away from some of the danger areas. Once at the open hatchway, getting into the craft is something of an art, requiring a nimble pull and push mantelshelf move with the arms as the floor is at about chest height. Rucsacs are carefully placed inside first. Once inside, communication is impossible without a headset or advanced gesticulation techniques, which the crews are always well versed in. You are normally told to sit in a specific seat, which is pointed out clearly (and to a newcomer apparently rudely, but that's just the way it has to be for safety and efficiency), and you then fasten the seat belt. The rest of the flight is just noise, though if you are lucky enough to get a view, you will be more than compensated. Getting out of the helicopter is again a matter of following instructions precisely, waiting your turn and hoping that you don't fall over after jumping out of the hatch. After scurrying, head crouched to a safe distance at the direction in which you have been pointed, you squat securely and await the wind blast from the machine's take off. Seconds later, peace returns and you realise that the weather is not too bad after all.

This basic training is then supplemented with experience at being winched into and out of the helicopter. This is much more fun and quite necessary, as there are occasions when the local terrain makes landing impossible and all personnel have to be winched in and out. The system is very simple. A thick sling is placed under the arms, a toggle pulled down to tighten it and up you go. Two rescuers can be raised at once, speeding things up considerably. Search dogs can also be raised aloft in pairs by similar means, though their respective temperaments need to match. One well known local incident in which two incompatible search dogs fought tooth and nail from ground level all the way to the helicopter fifty feet higher gave a whole new meaning to the phrase 'dog-fight' as applied to aeronautical situations.

If you are very lucky, you may have the opportunity to don a set of headphones and stand at the front to guide the pilot to the required location. This is an experience not to be missed. The visibility from the front of a Sea King is quite outstanding and the views of the fells you know so well are breathtaking. One thing that I was certainly not prepared for was the conversation which takes place between the crew members. Flying a machine with a value of millions rather than thousands would suggest that concentration has to be absolute, communications and navigation spot-on and the teamwork slick as an oil spill. Although there is no doubt that all this is true, one of my first experiences in a helicopter temporarily clouded that view.

We left Ambleside Rugby Club on a training flight, watched by a crowd which the club would have loved to have had for a match. I donned some headphones and stood clumsily at the front, tucking in behind the pilot, whilst the winchman showed me how to operate the speak switch. Initial chatter was technical, efficient, well practised. Once we were off the ground the conversation changed somewhat. What follows is as faithful a rendition as I can recall.

'Heading 150. Altitude 200. Wow, look at that one in the bikini down there!'

'Roger. Let's go back and get her number.'

'Where are we going . . .?'

'I don't know. Ask this guy here . . .'

'That's a nice place down there, wouldn't mind living there . . .'

'Nah, no night clubs.'

The conversation continued in a similar vein, technical necessi-
ties mixed with real laddish banter. It has to be said though, that
at all times I felt completely secure and relaxed, and had utter
confidence in all their abilities.

One session we were asked to organise was turned on its head
as it was the helicopter pilot who was being trained and assessed.
We positioned a casualty (my wife, Gill) in the sheepfolds at the
head of Scandale, and the pilot had a brief to search this and the
upper part of Rydale for the casualty site. I acted as a guide and
inevitably the search was successful – not through any personal
skills on my part I hasten to add – any four-year-old could have
spotted the phoney casualty, such is the unrivalled view from the
helicopter. We landed slightly rockily, loaded the stretcher and
flew back to the alternative landing site at Ambleside Cricket Club.
Once we had put down safely, the pilot shut down the engines and
we all met up outside the pavilion. He walked over to us and
removed his helmet. We must have looked quite a sight to him as
our jaws dropped and our eyes widened. The pilot looked all of
sixteen, just, and it was hard to believe he could have passed a
driving test, let alone flown the helicopter with such precision and
skill.

Helicopters are absolutely invaluable when it comes to searching. Not only are they able to transport groups of team members
to the appropriate locations quickly, but they offer an unparalleled
view down on to the ground. Believe me, there's no place to hide
if a helicopter is searching for you! Unfortunately, searching from
the air is not always possible due to high winds or low cloud –
common mountain conditions of course. The first rescue operation
in the country to make use of Global Positioning Systems also
involved helicopters in what can only be described as the ultimate
in high-tech rescues.

Modern GPS devices lock onto a number of satellites in order to verify the position of the user. They can give grid references, directions for getting to another location, a record of your route and a whole host of other fascinating, but utterly useless information. Their prices are becoming lower and lower, currently retailing at around £149 upwards, and they will soon be within the budget of many fell walkers. They are not inch perfect, though they could be, for a small random error is introduced by the US Military giving them approximately a six-figure grid reference accuracy which would put you within a hundred yards or so of your stated location. Potential buyers beware. This is not accurate enough to render conventional map and compass techniques obsolete, especially when you may be only fifty yards away from a large drop in whiteout conditions. Having said all this, I will certainly buy one when they are retailing at £49.95!

The first incident to use a GPS system involved a search for a group missing in the Pavey Ark area. The weather was extremely poor, with high winds, driving rain and a gently undulating cloud base which obscured the high fells. A good friend of mine, Bruce Corrie from the Kendal rescue team was one of a number of extra personnel who had been drafted in to assist in the search. His small group were to be the first to be airlifted onto the hill, and the helicopter crew were doubtful about the conditions. They put down on the flat area to the north of Pavey Ark, in the Thunacar Knott region, in atrocious conditions and winds so strong that the helicopter refused to place any more rescuers on the fell. However, as it turned back towards the valley, one of the crew glimpsed a flash of colour at the top of one of the many short gully lines on the east side of the crag. He used the helicopter's computer to fix an instant grid reference on the sighting and passed this on to Bruce's group before returning to Ambleside.

This scenario delighted Bruce, as he is both an able mountaineer and a technocrat of no mean intellect. Complex computer technology to him is like changing a spark plug to me, and I am certain he would have relished this high-tech approach to a rescue operation. He punched the appropriate grid reference into the GPS

169

device and fixed the position on the east side of the top of Pavey Ark on their map. Once they had reached a point close to their reference, they switched the machine on and allowed it to direct them. Whenever the pointer tried to get them to go into dangerous terrain, they simply crabbed sideways to another strike point until they could follow the arrow's direction again. When I asked Bruce about the final moment of the search, he described it as follows: 'We had to skirt around the top of several gullies to find the right point at which we could follow the direction given by the GPS, and as I was in the process of exclaiming that the missing group should be just about here ... there they were!' The technology provided by the helicopter and the GPS, coupled with some efficient rescue work and a lucky break in the clouds, brought a speedy end to what could have developed into a nightmare search.

Most rescuers take it for granted that the helicopter is a safe means of travel, yet this has been shown to be an optimistic way of looking at things. They do develop faults and they can crash, especially in the extremes of operational conditions they are likely to encounter in the hills. One such incident in the Lake District was particularly spectacular, yet no one was seriously hurt. The location was upper Eskdale, in my opinion, the finest part of the Lake District.

Most walkers approach the upper Esk from the unusually named Brotherilkeld, locally pronounced Butterilkeld, a farm which sits in the last flattening of the land before the grinding hairpins of Hardknott Pass. Easy walking leads to Throstlegarth, where the beck splits, Lingcove Beck flowing from the north-east and its source close to Ore Gap, the conspicuous low point between Bowfell and Esk Pike, whilst the main watercourse continues northwards towards the marshy wastes of The Great Moss. This section of river contains some magical pools, or 'dubs' as they are known, whose crystal clear waters appear translucent green and blue and dapple mystically in the summer sunshine, when they also provide natural swimming pools which have few equals outside those used in Tarzan films.

170

The Great Moss itself is a vast, flat area of wetland, ringed with high fells, whose ruggedness provides a stark contrast. The huge boulders of Samson Stones lie here, beneath the massive, broken buttress of Cam Spout. Slightly up valley lies one of the best climbing crags in the Lake District, Esk Buttress or Dow Crag as it is known on older maps, a gradually tapering sweep of pale dense granite. Between the two, steep water runnels tumble down from the highest ground in England beneath Scafell and Scafell Pike, and beyond them, the valley rises remorselessly to Esk Hause and the source of the River Esk. Few places in England can inspire such emotion and sense of splendid isolation as the Upper Esk, and even fewer can match its beauty.

The climbing hereabouts is amongst the finest in Britain. Above Esk Buttress and Cam Spout crags lie the bulky buttresses of Scafell itself, a Mecca for climbers and the very best of Lakeland crags. For many years, the mighty crags of Scafell held the hardest routes in the country. In 1903, Fred Botterill made an amazing lead on the slab which bears his name. Still a well respected Very Severe climb, he made the ascent in nailed boots and carried an ice axe. A little later, in 1914, came one of the most outstanding breakthroughs in the history of climbing. The huge Central Buttress of Scafell was climbed over two days by the powerful partnership of S. W. Herford and G. S. Sansom. Though they used a rope cradle to overcome the chockstone on the difficult Flake Crack, their ascent was way ahead of its time and the climb can rightly be credited as one which opened up a completely new era of climbing.

Many years and thousands of ascents later, the Central Buttress route was the scene of a tragic accident which was to alter the climb forever. The famous chockstone which had stood the test of time, and the pull of so many for so long, finally came out, possibly loosened by frost action or even by an earth tremor. In doing so, it injured a fine, young climber who was moving past it, causing bleeding which could not be stemmed in time to save his life. The ascent of the Great Flake has now been upgraded from Hard Very Severe to E2, a jump of two full grades.

It was lower down, on Cam Spout Crag that the climbing accident involving the helicopter occurred. As it edged closer and closer to the rock face, things seemed to be going well and the casualty had been clipped to the winchwire when, suddenly, a rotor blade touched the rock and its end snapped off. The helicopter became instantly destabilised and the pilot realised that he would have to attempt an emergency landing on the Great Moss. He manoeuvred the craft away from the cliff and down towards the welcome flatness of the Moss, but the casualty was still trailing out of the side door on the end of a winchwire! Frantic efforts were made inside the cabin to retract the wire, and the climber was hoisted aboard just before the impact of the crash landing. Miraculously, everyone came out of the incident alive, but one suspects that the pilot may have been a wee bit embarrassed to have to leave a million pounds worth of helicopter parked up on the wastes of the Great Moss.

Apart from any other factor, how were the RAF going to get it back? It was hard to envisage the necessary repairs being made on site! The answer was by lifting it out with another helicopter, this time one of those huge sinister-looking Chinooks with twin rotors. A large crowd had gathered to watch the operation, many no doubt expecting to see two helicopters stranded instead of one, but none of us should have underestimated the power of a Chinook, for in a few minutes of controlled strength it lifted the Sea King high above the swamp and started lumbering back to reunite it with its rightful owners.

Such are the good relations between RAF Boulmer pilots and the Lake District rescue teams, that we have sometimes been offered lifts on their training exercises. Martin Scrowston and I are probably the only two people to have had a downhill walk to climb on the Scafell cliffs, after getting deposited by helicopter near the summit of Scafell itself. Access to these crags is normally hard won after a steep slog up Brown Tongue from Wasdale, but not this time, when a gentle fifteen minute descent brought us to the foot of the crag. We also procured a ride to the top of Pavey Ark, where

John Barlow, a genial paragliding instructor from Coniston, and I flew back down to the valley by paraglider. These incidents were rare, but real treats, and offer one of the few perks of the job.

We have also used helicopter assistance for sheep rescues. If the crew need to put in some training hours, it makes sense for them to be involved in some sort of rescue operation, even if it only involves a cerebrally deficient Herdwick ewe. The most memorable incident of this kind came when we were asked to remove two sheep from high on the Bowfell crags. Though not averse to walking up and down, it was a much better use of everyone's time to carry out the rescue by helicopter. After being picked up at Ambleside Rugby Club, we flew out to the head of Langdale and swept the cliffs which line the Langdale rim of the summit – Bowfell Buttress, Cambridge Crags, and Flat Rock. It was absurdly simple work to pick out the stranded ewes, making a mockery of the time it can take to assess the situation from below. The pilot picked out a landing site near to the top of Bowfell Buttress, where the most difficult location lay, and after the winchman, leaning from the side door, had guided us gently down, the pilot simply parked the machine on the spot and waited for us to finish.

The rescue took about twenty-five minutes, after which we loped back to the landing site, reboarded and were taken to the second location at the opposite end of the mountain. A rapid fifteen-minute operation here and we were back on board. Ten minutes later we landed in Ambleside. It had taken about an hour and a half to perform an operation which conventionally would have taken the best part of a day, with the additional benefits of some useful training practice for the crew, the gaining of considerable goodwill from the farming community and a real treat for the walkers on Bowfell, none of whom would have expected to turn the brow of the hill and come across a Sea King helicopter parked up as casually as you might park your car in a town centre multi-storey.

It is a common belief, and one I share, that accidents are most likely to happen when we least expect them. This is particularly true in the outdoors, when one mistake can have such serious consequences. Edward Whymper summed it all up with his famous observation: 'Climb if you will, but remember that courage and strength are naught without prudence and that a momentary negligence could cost the happiness of a lifetime. Do nothing in haste, look well to each step, and from the beginning, think what may be the end.'

When danger is all around us, we take extra care. As soon as the perceived danger has elapsed, we drop our guard and become vulnerable to dangers we had previously not even considered. Such was the situation on a call-out to the steep path which works its way up the edge of Hell Gill at the head of Oxendale. It's an appropriately named spot, dark and dank, vertical-sided and frequently alive with a torrent of foaming water. The lower sector rises through as steep a fellside as any local path ascends before it eases to grassy slopes which rise into a gentle V-shaped valley, before a final steepening to join the main track to Three Tarns at the top of the Band.

The incident reported was a collapse, always a worrying scenario, in which little accurate information is normally available and the consequences of a lengthy wait for treatment potentially serious. Luckily, in this case, a helicopter was in the area and it landed swiftly at Ambleside rugby ground to pick up me, our so-called 'micromedic', Dr Sarah Hollis, (under five feet tall but packs a lot into it), team leader Stewart Hulse (whose robust stature and extensive first aid experience make him our 'macromedic'), a couple of other members, a stretcher and first aid equipment. We were above the scene in minutes, and the helicopter manoeuvred into position with a precision born of years of demanding practice and experience. It touched down gently on a flatter area of land, close to the edge of the ghyll itself and just above the path's steep descent. We were on easy terrain with no perceptible danger to watch out for, except the usual fear of being decapitated by the helicopter's rotors or set on fire by its exhaust. However, we were taken by surprise as we jumped out of the side door, landed on soft grass, and made our way downhill, away from the immediate danger area, which our training had taught us was the helicopter itself.

It was Sarah who quickly found out the hidden problem. It was a windy day and, coupled with this, the downdraught from the helicopter's rotors was so severe that an incredible wind blew down the slope towards the edge of the gorge. As soon as Sarah stood up and started to jog down the fellside, the wind pushed jog to run and run to sprint, and she hurtled out of control towards the edge of Hell Gill, as if intending to leap clean across to the other side. Stewart and I reacted instinctively, and managed to rugby tackle her to the ground before she went over the side. It was a very dangerous moment, which had sprung out of nothing, and a sharp reminder of the fact that danger lurks in so many unexpected places and at so many seemingly innocuous times.

11

FALCONS
IN FLIGHT

Although the flight of a helicopter is a quite outstanding feat of engineering, nothing man can achieve is able to compete with the wonders of flight provided in the natural world, perhaps exemplified best by birds of prey. I recall quite vividly the first time I saw a peregrine falcon at close quarters. I had been working with the National Park's Ranger Service for just a couple of months, when Spider Penman, the Ranger for Langdale at the time, took me up into Easedale. I don't mind admitting that Spider was something of a hero to me at the time. He was doing the job which I aspired to, and he was an outstanding climber, with a fine array of colourful stories to match. Well liked by most and held in high esteem by many, here was a man who was an ideal role model for a young trainee like myself.

He was lean and fit and in those early days I remember struggling to keep up with Spider on rough descents from steep fellsides, despite being relatively competent myself, and being amazed that he could wear a hefty pair of Alpine-style climbing boots virtually all the time, even for driving. I recall him turning out for work one day in a pair of bright blue glossy plastic boots, the forerunner of modern plastic mountaineering footwear. As we drove into Langdale to repair some stiles, we pulled in to the side of the road before the New Dungeon Ghyll.

'Have to test these out, John,' said Spider, as we sprinted up to Lower Scout Crag, a popular beginner's climbing location on Langdale. The test he had in mind was to solo a fifty-foot climb, then known as the Moving Chockstone, which I had not done before. Spider swarmed up the glassy slab and climbed smoothly past the crux, a series of delicate moves on polished and slippery holds, dealing competently with the numbness of his stiff and ungainly boots. He paused to warn me that the handhold moved a little, before quickly pulling over onto the top of the crag to await my effort. Still very much a beginner, I climbed slowly and carefully, and after much deliberating about the delicacy of the slab, I reached the big handhold and leaned back on it. Yes, I had been warned that it moved a little, but suddenly to find that the whole block pulled out several inches once it was weighted was enough to double my heart rate and spur me on to conclude the climb in a fraction of the time I expected. Spider just grinned. 'Not bad, these boots.'

From that day, I took great delight in introducing friends who were new to climbing in the area to the delights of the Moving Chockstone route. We would hang from the stone itself on one hand, laughing at its preposterous movement, or caress it gently as we passed, waiting for the momentary panic as the visiting climber fleetingly thought his time was up as the hold moved, but then topped reliably. I have to admit to being a little disturbed, though, when some years later I wandered up to the crag to solo the same route on the way up to climb on White Ghyll Crag. The moving chockstone had gone and in its place was a neat triangular recess. All the times we had swung and pulled on it, laughing and joking, and all the time it must have been so close to depositing us on the rocky ground forty feet below. I always wondered what happened. It is unlikely that anyone fell to the ground whilst swinging audaciously from it, as that would certainly have resulted in severe injury or worse and we would have known. My best guess is that it was levered from its home by some well-meaning individual who thought it dangerous and that others could not be entrusted to make their own decisions regarding its security. If anyone wants to own up to such a misguided action, I would welcome the story – and so would Spider!

I remember little of our walk up to Easedale Tarn that day, though it was probably as pleasantly innocuous and mediocre as it is now, with its manicured paths and virtually constant stream of walkers. Once at the tarn, however, the area reveals more of its true character. Gentle grassy fellsides stretch out to huge mounds of moraine, strewn with bracken and dotted with rough boulders. These steepen inexorably towards the back wall of this upper valley which is ringed with sombre crags, streaked grey, black and green. Few openings for paths exist and even the trade route to Codale Tarn has several rocky steps which require care. Spider took me up to one side of the tarn, to a vantage point from where we could get a fine view of the surrounding crags. He firstly singled out the right cliff for me, then, using colours and shapes on the rock as pointers, he showed me the position of an ancient eagle's nest, described as being 'as big as a Mini'. Falcons may have been nesting here, or on ledges above.

We would find out. The approach to the crag was arduous, meandering in and out of huge humps of ancient moraine, though it was broken by one momentary and marvellous incident, when we saw a weasel chasing a pipit up a dry stream bed. The tiny weasel danced and flitted from stone to stone, and appeared to mesmerise the bird, which slowly hopped along seemingly oblivious to the danger it faced. Our presence broke the spell of the moment, and the bird sprang to the wing in a flash, whilst the cunning weasel glanced back at us as if to say 'thanks a lot', before dashing into the bracken.

We were threading our way past a series of outcrops of rough igneous rock, aiming for the top left-hand edge of the main buttress when, suddenly, an anchor-shaped slaty blue bird sliced through the air close by us in an unparalleled display of streamlined flight.

178

It swept gracefully up towards the cliff top and, with the lightest flutter of wing feather adjustment, it landed in an old rowan tree, turned its head and glared at us. Its upper back and wings appeared hunched upwards, almost vulture-like, a measure of its power and speed, and an indication of its character. Any other comparisons with vultures end abruptly, as the peregrine is master of the air, and possesses a speed of flight and an aerobatic capacity virtually unmatched. This particular falcon appeared unphased by our approach and allowed us to within thirty yards before issuing its harsh kekking call and taking off to circle the air above us. Its flight was quite breathtaking, and I stared in wonder as Spider located the nesting site with his binoculars. The chicks were ensconced in the middle of the old eagle's nest, two of them, dirty grey-white and huddled together like frightened children. To avoid disturbing the birds, we left immediately and jogged back down to the tarn, where the wild cries of the falcon were camouflaged by the screeching black-headed gulls who had made the tarn their home. My first falcon encounter was over, but fortunately it was to be the first of many.

Like other birds of prey, falcons suffered terrible losses in the 'fifties, 'sixties and 'seventies as a result of the extensive use of pesticides such as DDT. Its main food was the humble pigeon, many of which fed on contaminated corn and other seed. The pollutants built up in the pigeons, and these concentrated doses built up even more in the peregrine, its position at the very end of the food chain guaranteeing this. The results will probably be familiar to many readers. Eggs were infertile, or thin-shelled and broke before hatching. Populations declined startlingly and in the mid 1960s there were only a couple of nesting pairs left in the Lake District. Their decline continued throughout Europe and they quickly became an endangered species. A ban on the use of many of the offending pesticides led to a partial recovery, but by now the peregrine had become a valuable commodity. Clutches of eggs were a sought after item. The thief or collector would watch the eyrie and wait for the first egg to be laid, substituting a chicken's

179

egg for it, to ensure each individual egg of the clutch was collected while it was as clean as possible. This process would continue until all the eggs had been collected and the falcon (the name for the female peregrine – the male is known as the tiercel) was left sitting on a worthless collection. A clutch of falcon's eggs was, and still is, a prized possession amongst those who value such things, though collecting them is now not only highly illegal, but also, in my opinion, a morally corrupt and completely worthless activity.

In addition to this, the birds themselves are extremely valuable, and in the early 1980s a chick could be sold for around £1500. A clutch of healthy young falcons was therefore a rewarding prize. Adults could also fetch high prices, and traps were found at several Lake District nesting sites, where a tethered pigeon and net could lure an adult bird into captivity. Many of these trapped and stolen birds were sold to falconers as far away as Germany and Saudi Arabia, where their hunting skills are much prized.

Falcons have another enemy nearer home. Pigeons make a good meal for a falcon, especially the strong racing type with plenty of meat on them. Fanciers from West Cumbrian towns such as Maryport and Workington would send their prize birds out to race back home, but their route would take them over the Lake District fells, where they stopped being racing birds and simply became a fast food takeaway for the peregrines. Many a fine racer has been lost like this and in my many visits to falcon nesting sites I have seen hundred upon hundred of the identifying rings which are placed around the pigeon's legs, sometimes with the leg, but little else, still attached. With the high number of falcons breeding in the area now, the racing pigeon is an important part of their staple diet, and the current population is maintained at an artificially high level due to this abundance of food which would not naturally be available. Small wonder some local pigeon fanciers are upset enough with falcons to want to destroy their nesting sites.

As in all ecosystems, the success of one species is the decline of another. Ravens, which naturally occupy similar nesting sites to the falcons, have suffered as a direct result of competition for breeding sites, and ring ouzels, which typically occupy the scree slopes beneath the crags, seem to be in decline as a result of the predatory nature of the falcon.

It is worth mentioning briefly the method by which the peregrine catches and kills much of its prey. The main method is called the 'stoop', a high-speed dive in which the hunting falcon folds back its wings and drops out of the sky at incredible speeds. Just before impact with its unfortunate victim, it extends its talons and literally knocks its prey out of the sky. The impact is such that death tends to be instantaneous, and only if you have seen a stoop take place can you really appreciate the speed and power of the hunter. Another method I have seen is for the falcon to catch an ailing bird from behind, and simply grab it from above as it flies past and carry it away to be killed at the next stop. Always, it is the speed, power and the precision of flight that is so amazing. Prey may then be taken to plucking sites, often grass-topped knolls above favourite crags with a good vantage point. The victim is defeathered and either devoured or taken to a food storage site to be used later. Almost always the evidence of a kill is the same – a neat circular pattern of small feathers and down, about two or three feet in diameter.

To combat threats to the peregrine's existence in Lakeland, the National Park, the British Trust for Ornithology and a rather shapeless and independent group calling themselves the North West Protection Group joined forces with other volunteers to create an organised deterrent to the thieves. Particularly vulnerable sites were watched round the clock, but to the embarrassment of the watchers, in some instances, this did not prevent the theft of eggs or young, as thieves slipped in during periods of misty weather when the crags were not visible.

The falcon is predominantly a cliff-nester and, as many of the sites were on crags which also attracted climbers, Spider Penman started a scheme which aimed to inform the climbing public when they were on a route which ventured too close to a nest and might cause disturbance. This involved the National Park's signwriter (a likeable and highly skilled youth who assisted us in making an exceedingly fast sledge, but that's another story) making small signs which we would hang up above the start of the climb, so that only the climber making the ascent could read them. The signs read something like this: 'Peregrines nesting. Please avoid X route and Y route until the end of July. Thanks.' The informality of the signs, their position, and the fact that they had been placed there by a climber who was also a conservationist meant that they were largely successful.

A variety of individuals from the interested organisations also joined forces to record nesting sites and their contents systematically, so that an accurate record could be obtained of the number of pairs breeding, and the number of sites which were being interfered with. One of the main men in this operation was Terry Pickford. A suave and neatly turned out character, Terry defies the stereotype of the ornithologist, often looking as if he has just walked off a film set rather than off the fell. Having said this, he knew his stuff and he had a real sixth sense for locating falcons, some of which rubbed off on me. My first encounter with Terry came after I was given the task of going out with him to a falcon eyrie so that the eggs could be marked with an infra red pen. Terry could abseil already and my presence was really to ensure that it was all nice and safe.

I arranged some belays for him and threw the rope over the edge of the crag. I was happy to leave the rest to him, when I noticed that the line he had taken on the upper part of the abseil meant that the rope was running at an angle before it dropped down the rock face. It was painfully obvious that at some stage the rope was likely to spring suddenly back to a straight line, putting extra strain on the anchors and running the risk of rope damage as it slid tensioned over the rough rock. I politely pointed this out to Terry, who was by now well into his James Bond stuntman routine, to be greeted with an 'it'll be OK' type comment. A few seconds later Terry was suspended in space about a hundred feet above the ground when the rope twanged. The rope and anchors were

182

undamaged, but as the rope slipped, it dropped him a couple of feet, just enough to simulate that momentary feeling of impending doom. His terrified yell was quite sufficient to let me know that he would listen to me on the next occasion. For several years I looked after Terry on the crags, ensuring that his descents were safe, and on occasions doing the work for him when the situation was too demanding.

The main thrust of this part of the protection scheme was to mark the eggs and the chicks with an infra red dye, whose formula was specific to each eyrie visited. In this way, when the authorities located stolen eggs or chicks, it would be possible to prove beyond doubt which eyrie they had come from. The secondary aim was to record the nesting sites, check on numbers and ascertain which sites were being raided.

The overall result of this work and that of many other professionals and volunteers is that the falcon population in the Lake District has steadily increased to levels which are higher than the pre-war figures. Peregrines now compete for nesting sites not just with ravens but with each other, and it is generally held that the present population of something around seventy pairs is artificially high, due in the main to the extra food available courtesy of the pigeon fanciers. The central fells became particularly important, containing what I believe to be the highest breeding density of peregrines in the world, and establishing the Lake District as a premier breeding site of international status. Some of our falcons were even taken to Czechoslovakia to help reinstate their ailing population.

One of the oddest rescues I have undertaken involved recovering a falcon chick which fled the nest a little too soon. It was particularly embarrassing as it jumped from 300 feet as Terry descended to mark and ring it in front of the *Naturewatch* TV programme cameras! For some time, we had been involved in filming a *Naturewatch* programme looking at peregrines with Julian Pettifer, who was a great person to work with, professional, genuinely interested and very friendly. One of the sites we visited was at White Scar, a huge limestone crag on the edge of Whitbarrow Scar, overlooking the Kent estuary. It was one of the most intimidating locations I have been to in this country, consisting of a towering natural escarpment, poised above a couple of hundred feet of scree and quarry workings, giving a total abseil length of almost 400 feet, the lower section of which was so loose as to be incredibly dangerous. We arrived early in the morning, and arranged the camera locations, fastening one particularly adventurous character right on to the edge of the void, where he stayed for several hours. When everything was set up, Terry and I hiked to the top of the cliff and located a stout hawthorn bush to set up the abseil from. Terry prepared to descend, somewhat nervously I have to add, and the cameras rolled. However, on reaching the nesting site, its sole occupant took one look at Terry, decided he wasn't mum and jumped.

To describe its descent as flight would be inaccurate, a faltering glide would be more realistic, yet it managed to reach an area of woodland several hundred feet lower and a few hundred yards away from the foot of the cliffs. We feared the embarrassing worst, and immediately marked the location and descended to try to find it, desperately hoping that it was still in one piece. Fifteen minutes searching resulted in success, and the location of an uninjured, but disorientated and, no doubt, most upset chick. We placed it in a black cloth bag, and it settled down for the next part of its adventure, getting back to the nest. As quickly as possible, we took it back to the cliff top, and I descended by abseil with it in a rucsac. The eyrie was easy to reach, and I carefully placed it back in the nest and vacated the place with a giant swing out on the rope so as to disturb it as little as possible. However, the worst was yet to come and I have to confess to being as frightened on this abseil as any, not only due to the fact that it was so long, and we had to borrow a special length rope, but that there was such a huge amount of loose rock and debris which could have been dislodged by the rope above me at any time, with potentially serious results, making me feel as though I should be wearing several helmets and a full suit of body armour. Rocks whizzed and whistled past like gunfire, and I got off the rope at the foot of the crag truly relieved that I was unhurt. That the falcon chick was happily returned to its eyrie was just a bonus.

The filming continued in a variety of locations, one of the most amazing being a huge quarry which was still working. We crept along an old tunnel which finished half way up one side of the quarry, from where it was possible to film across to the eyrie which was around fifty feet from the ground. Blasting work was still in progress on a daily basis and we watched explosions send great clods of slate high above the sitting falcon and only a few yards to the side. I knew that falcons are a tolerant species, but to thrive in an environment which resembled the Blitz was quite extraordinary.

Monitoring the increasingly numerous nesting sites of the peregrine was one of the most rewarding parts of my job, and left many indelible memories. I was up in the Coppermines valley, above Coniston, one day, when I received a message on my radio asking me to go to Raven Crag, Yewdale, where there had been a problem with a climber disturbing a pair of nesting falcons. Wilful disturbance of the birds is quite a serious offence, punishable by a hefty fine and it was clear from the radio message that the person who had reported the incident (who turned out to be Terry Pickford) was going for the jugular and wanted a prosecution. The climber involved was none other than Chris Bonington and he was climbing with another famous climbing name, the author Tony Greenbank. I knew that there was absolutely no way that either would have knowingly disturbed the birds.

Yewdale was only ten minutes away, and I arrived to find a rather frosty situation in which Terry was clearly not satisfied that Bonington was entirely innocent. Attempting to defuse the situation with humour and friendliness, I asked Chris if he had managed to get one of the chicks, and if so, how much did he want for it? Terry was not amused by this. Chris then explained what had happened. The route they had been climbing took a line which passed just a few feet to the side of the peregrine's nest. They had just got this high on the climb when Terry had seen them and cautioned them. When peregrines are nesting, the mother will not leave the nest until the source of the disturbance is very close indeed. So Chris and Tony could have had no prior knowledge of the nest site, and I'm sure it must have come as quite a shock when the falcon shot vociferously off its ledge and proceeded to admonish the intruders with its swooping dive and incessant harsh kekking noise. When all this happened, Chris was established on the top pitch of the route, with Tony belayed on a small ledge about seventy feet above the ground. It was clear that, in the circumstances, it would have been far more time-consuming and difficult to have retreated than to continue swiftly to the top. To a non-climber the mechanics of the sport and the detail of what is feasible and what is not can be confusing. Terry no doubt thought that retreat was an easy option, whilst Chris and Tony probably wished that they could have had Terry on the end of a rope one hundred feet off the ground to persuade him otherwise. An eventual truce was reached and the incident became as insignificant as it had in reality been in the first place.

The valley of Rydale is far less frequented than the fine ridges of the Fairfield Horseshoe which enclose it, and a good thing too. It is calming, tranquil and varied in its lower part, bearing such gems as the natural weir at Buckstones Jump, but wild and breathtakingly desolate in its upper reaches. The track which ascends the true right side of the valley bottom was the scene of the most dramatic landslide I have ever seen in the area. A bank of fellside several feet deep and about fifty yards long slid across the track, temporarily blocking it and demolishing a couple of huge sections of wall on the way down to the beck. This might not seem that exceptional, but on viewing it, the most startling factor was the gentle angle of the ground on which the landslide had taken place, which I would estimate to be no more than about 15 degrees.

Beyond this point lies the largest crag of the dale, Erne Crag. Erne is the old name for a sea eagle, and it is likely that in the distant past, a pair occupied a nesting site here. In more recent times it has been a regular falcon nesting site and a well-known one at that, from which eggs and chicks have been stolen several times. One potential thief got more than he bargained for when, in an attempt to reach the eyrie, he fell a considerable distance and sustained serious multiple injuries, a harsh justice. Further up the valley is a delightful yet almost unvisited buttress known as Black Crag. Falcons may also nest here, and on one memorable evening when I was checking the local nesting sites by climbing down from the crag top, I peered over a small bulge of rock to see the falcon sitting on her 'scrape' (the name given to a nesting site in an earthy hollow in a ledge, as opposed to a nest), not a yard below me. It took a few moments for her to realise I was there, and she just turned and stared hard before remonstrating most vocally, at which point I made a hurried retreat. As I scrambled away, the falcon buzzed me several times, diving close by in a series of complex spirals before swirling away, kekking as she gained height in order to glide back to her chicks.

Snatched moments such as this with some of our more remark-able wildlife are few and far between, yet forged from such fleeting encounters are indelible and precious memories. In another falcon search in the Wasdale area, a fruitless day brought a sudden and completely unexpected reward at its end. I had one final crag to check, an insignificant and broken affair at which I held little hope of finding anything. Approaching it from above over a gradually steepening fellside, each level of rock only revealed itself upon very close acquaintance, due to the convex shape of the slope. One section of crag looked steeper than the rest, so I headed casually for it and scrambled down over some blocky steps onto a narrow bilberry ledge. I glanced down, and to my utter amazement, not ten feet below me was an enormous nest, upon which sat a magnificent golden eagle. I really could not believe my eyes. After casting me a wary backward glance, the eagle stood up and stepped off the eyrie, feathered his wingtips and glided across to the far side of the valley, his mastery of the air being so complete that he covered the distance without even a single wingbeat. All the hard walking of several years, the wet days, the cold ones and every conceivable disappointment was rendered entirely worthwhile by this one majestic moment.

Others have not been so lucky. The lure of rare birds of prey is such that people have been hurt both in the process of attempting to take chicks, and when merely wanting to get an innocent closer look. The Lake District's resident eagles normally nest at a well known location in the Haweswater area, heavily guarded by the RSPB. The nesting site is likely to be on steep craggy fellsides which see few if any casual walkers, so the terrain is pathless and the rock dirty, heavily vegetated and slippery. In an apparent attempt to get a closer view of the eagles, one walker tragically fell to his death here, such is the treacherous nature of the terrain most birds of prey nest amongst.

The nesting site in Easedale previously mentioned was also the location for some of the *Naturewatch* filming. A hide was constructed and some excellent film taken. After the hide was dismantled, I visited the crag with one of the country's leading botanists, Dr Bob Bunce. A specialist in mountain flora, Bob has an enviable ability to communicate even the most detailed and complex information in a manner which makes sense even to a layman like myself. That day in Easedale, Bob and I had explored virtually every nook and cranny of the cliff which might conceal a hidden flush of botanical fascination and had seen nothing at all of particular interest. Yet as we scrambled down a series of rock ledges beneath the main buttress, Bob paused and stared at a tight clump of vegetation which lay partially concealed beneath a small overhang. I noticed his eyes widen and I could sense his increasing pulse and the intensity of his glare. Puzzled to the point of annoyance, he pointed out some dull leathery leaves, the likes of which he had not seen before. Sensing a new discovery, perhaps a plant he could give his name to – Saxifragus Buncus, for example – he clambered impatiently down for closer examination.

'Bob,' I shouted, 'I know what it is!' He looked at me doubtfully. How could I possibly know something the great man did not? His excited inspection continued and, as he crouched down on the ledge, prepared for a detailed examination, I found it hard to conceal a smile. He looked up and laughed out loud. The mysterious undiscovered species was a section of old camouflage netting!

One final ornithological encounter worthy of note occurred in the ancient Caledonian forests of Scots pine near Loch Garten, which is of course internationally renowned for its ospreys. Birds of prey may be fierce, but I can assure you that nothing matches the ferocity of the bird in this chance meeting. I was taking a walk late in the day through some wonderful pine forest which allowed the mellow evening sunshine to spread fingers of warmth through onto the carpet of old needles which covered its damp floor. As in some enchanted forest from a mythical tale, the silence and beauty of the woodland bewitched me, and for a few moments I could have been in a different world completely. My dream-like state was abruptly disturbed, however, when a large black bird speared a flightpath towards me from one side and landed about twenty yards away. My initial thoughts were that it was surprising that a crow or suchlike would have come so close but, on closer examination, this bird was bigger and bulkier than any crow I had seen. As it peered at me through the long strands of heather, I recognised it – a capercaillie! Though no doubt relatively common in the Highlands, this was my first sighting, and I determined to remain still and see as much as I could.

Hardly breathing, I watched the bird come a little closer, weaving its way from side to side through the clumps of grass and heather, lowering its head, then peering quizzically at me as if making a thorough examination. I remained as motionless as I was able, and the bird approached closer. I gradually realised how large it was, perhaps the size of a small turkey, but certainly large enough to make a substantial impression and with a hooked beak which appeared designed to hurt. I watched, spellbound as it continued its approach, and I remained determined to keep as still as possible in order to get the best view.

By now, it had started to issue a deep throaty croak which

increased in intensity and volume the closer it approached. Before I knew it, the bird was just a couple of yards away and I still hadn't clicked that the bird was just as interested in me as I was in it. Then, with no warning, it leapt at me, flapping its wings and attempting to spear my leg with its blunt pincer-like bill. It was only then I had the sense to turn tail and I ran as if being chased by a pride of lions. After a fifty metre sprint that would have done Linford Christie proud, I turned, expecting to have left the aggress-ive over-grown grouse behind. It took a few micro seconds for my eyes to adjust to the shock of seeing what looked like a miniature Stealth bomber homing in at high velocity on my head. To avoid what would have been a direct hit, I had to leap nimbly to one side, turning to see the capercaillie preparing to round on me once more.

This time I was determined to be prepared and, picking up a stout length of stick, I hid behind the nearest tree trunk and prepared for battle. It adopted similar tactics to the first time, approaching in a haphazard, meandering way, threading a path through the twiggy stems of heather until it was close enough for a strike. As it plunged at me a third time, I gently fended it off with the stick, moving from side to side behind the tree as it tried remorselessly to inflict as much damage as it was able. Realising that it was not going to become fed up and fly away into the darkness of the forest, I decided that by sprinting from tree to tree, I might be able to escape unhurt. What a casual observer would have made of the sight of a grown man racing from tree to tree, pursued relentlessly by a black turkey I can only guess, but fortunately the forest was ours alone, and once I was out of its strictly guarded territory, it cackled its victory and continued its drunken-looking waddle back into the forest.

Some weeks later, my neighbour, to whom I had recounted the tale, came back from a holiday in Galloway where he had spoken to an RSPB warden working at a local reserve. The warden had also worked in the past at the Loch Garten site, which resulted in the story of my capercaillie encounter being recounted yet again.

My neighbour then learned that I was not the first to be assailed by this intimidating menace, and that its ferocity was well documented, in particular as a local forestry worker had his arm broken by it! You have been warned!

12

SETTING
THE STANDARDS

As the number of rescue incidents has increased over the last few years, so has the need for team members to be trained to increasingly high levels. An examination of the skills required to cope with the Jim incidents mentioned earlier – which were all relatively simple – is quite illuminating. Each incident required the efficient use of the team's communication system, so radio procedure has to be professional and speech concise and accurate. We have to learn where 'dead spots' are – the areas in which communication with base becomes impossible – and we have to learn how to set up relays and where the best locations for them are. Much of this comes down to the sort of local knowledge which can only spring from experience. After the call-out has been instigated, the team has to identify the best access point from which to tackle the incident, and this may not necessarily be the location from which the informant has raised the alarm. Again, good local knowledge and sound judgement provide the answer. Good navigational skills are required to make certain that both team members and their equipment get to the right location via the fastest route. In bad conditions, locating the casualty site can be difficult, in fact locating anything can be difficult if the conditions are bad enough.

There was an embarrassing incident at one of Langdale's country fairs a few years ago. The event was being held at Stool End Farm, and a fine array of tents, marquees, vehicles and stalls sprawled across the large field in front of the farmhouse. A fell race had been organised as part of the proceedings and, though unimaginative in its route, it was certain to provide a testing run as the line it took was more or less direct from the farm, up the valley of Oxendale and then straight up to the summit of Shelter Crags. Viewed in cross-section, the route appears almost as an hyperbolic curve and the climb out of the head of Oxendale, up Whorneyside breast and then to the summit was a guaranteed lung-bursting muscle-shredder. The team had agreed to place a man on the summit to count the runners as they went past and ensure all reached the high point, but on the day a thick swirling mist had enveloped the top thousand feet of the fell. It would be unfair to disclose the name of the young team member who took on this responsibility, but I should thank him for giving us one of the best laughs we've ever had.

A small group of rescuers were waiting with a team Land Rover on the show site to demonstrate the workings of various items of equipment and to promote mountain safety to the hundreds of visitors the show had attracted. Our budding fell-running rescuer, who I'll call Simon, had a radio, and was able to communicate freely with us. He left the show field an hour and a half or so before the race started, and provided us with a periodic burst of crackling over the handset from which we could decipher his progress. By the time the famous Billy Bland had led the field of runners out of the farmyard, Simon was high on Crinkle Crags, but somewhat unsure of his position. By the time Billy Bland had muscled his way to a midway point on the race, Simon had still not located the summit, and was getting desperate – as would anyone who knew the speed at which Billy Bland ran. The radio messages became more frequent and more panic stricken.

'I'm on a path,' said Simon.

'Yes,' said we. 'Can you see any distinguishing features?'

There was a pause for a minute, until a breathless voice almost sobbed over the radio, 'Yes, yes . . . There's a cairn in front of me!'

This was the cue for uncontrollable laughter amongst all present, and the cruellest advice of all – 'Why don't you wait until someone comes past and ask them!'

Simon's messages became increasingly broken and unreadable, though we were never sure exactly why, and when Billy Bland led the field home he reported that the rescuer on the summit was conspicuous only by his absence.

I'm sure we all felt a little sympathy for Simon but, on a serious note, if a rescuer can't find his or her way about on the fells in poorish visibility during the daytime, you really have to question that person's suitability for rescue work. In my opinion, all rescuers should be able to navigate accurately in whatever conditions the weather may throw at them, day or night, as a fundamental prerequisite. The inability to do this could be dangerous to the point of being life-threatening.

Other skills required on the Jim incidents include the ability to assess the casualty's condition and carry out the necessary first aid, including giving intra-muscular injections. Those present may also have to assemble the stretcher, operate specialist first aid equipment such as the back splint, administer Entonox, or assist in the carry down the fellside. Each and every one of these skills has to be gained through both training and practice. Training sessions can cover virtually anything to do with rescue work, from advanced first aid to advanced driving, from stretcher lowers to treating heart conditions and administering drugs intravenously.

However, almost all rescue team members face one major disadvantage. No matter how many rescues they attend, they will never get the continuous practice at each skill which, for example, a paramedic or a professional rescuer in the Alps would get. This fact places considerable stress on team members when they are faced with medical situations which they must approach with a great degree of circumspection. Mountain rescuers may have to deal with heart attacks, multiple injuries, internal or serious head injuries and unknown medical conditions which might tax the facilities of an Accident and Emergency Unit in a hospital, let alone the limited skills, equipment and experience available to a rescue team high on a hostile mountainside, where an incorrect diagnosis and treatment could mean loss of life.

From a medical point of view, the Langdale/Ambleside team has probably done more than any other to improve the first aid skills of its members to a level which starts to approach those of the professionals in this field. Much of this is due to the attitude and push provided by Stewart Hulse. His view is that the medical profession cloaks itself in mystique and complexity in a deliberate effort to alienate the layman, and to some extent I agree with him. He argues that many of the routine matters attended to by nurses and doctors, such as setting up an IV drip, are well within the capabilities of a number of team members, and that acquiring these skills would enhance the service we are able to provide to the public. Stewart is all for demystifying the medical profession, and is determined that the Langdale/Ambleside team should be at the forefront of medical development in mountain rescue. His resilience and stubborn nature have probably played a major part in the evolution of this process, and in recent years the medical equipment in the team's possession has become increasingly complex and task-specific, at the same time as the training has become increasingly thorough and increasingly directed at a higher level of ability. A nucleus of team members who are frequently first or near first on the scene has been given special training in the administering of drugs, setting up drips and so on.

My only worry relates to that well-known saying about a little knowledge being a dangerous thing. The first aid skills that rescuers are being taught will no doubt prove a vital part of the successful treatment of many casualties, but if the response of the casualty proves not to be as anticipated, I wonder whether the lack of training in depth and diagnostic skills might prove a major stumbling block in certain isolated cases.

It is a surprise to many people outside rescue work just how complex some of the medical equipment used by teams has become, particularly bearing in mind the fact that although doctors may be present in some circumstances, this is by no means guaranteed, leaving the work to be done by amateurs with limited training. The defibrillator is a good example. This is a piece of equipment which will be familiar to anyone who watches TV programmes such as *Casualty* or *Cardiac Arrest*. It's the one where everyone rushes about and shouts as two large pads with handles are placed over the casualty's chest, someone shouts 'Clear' and 'Shock' and the body quivers on the table as the camera zooms in on the faces of the stars, who portray anguish or relief, depending upon the result. The defib provides an electric shock which can stimulate the heart into resuming normal rhythm in cases where it has either stopped completely or has settled into an abnormal pattern. It is a potential life-saver, and the version used by rescue teams is portable. The major problem, as always in rescue work, is the time delay between the incident occurring and the team arriving. In cases of heart attacks, this delay often means that we have absolutely no realistic chance of helping the casualty. This is a sad fact, as in recent years, the number of heart attacks suffered on the fells has increased dramatically. Although, to my knowledge, no one has yet been revived successfully from a heart attack using the defibrillator in a mountain rescue call-out, no doubt there will come a time when it is successful, and in the meantime it offers a useful way of monitoring the condition of those who have suffered non-fatal heart problems.

Operation of the equipment is relatively simple. Two sticky pads attach the electrodes to the casualty's chest and the machine provides a visual ECG readout. It also advises whether it thinks that a shock is necessary, though it is possible to override this advice. The ECG readout can also be printed out. The information given by the unit is complex, and can in reality only be effectively diagnosed by an appropriate specialist, but in cases where the patient's heart has stopped, a shock can be applied by team members quite easily. The ECG printout can also be sent for a specialist to view via the portable fax machine. This high-tech box of electronic wizardry can whoosh a fax from the fellsides to a doctor anywhere in the country. In this way, a specialist could examine an ECG or other information and offer immediate advice on treatment to the rescuers, who could then act on the best advice. The machine also provides an ongoing record of the casualty's condition, which may be important at a later stage in their treatment.

I have been involved in the use of the defib just once, and it left me with mixed feelings. An elderly man had collapsed at the bottom of the Easedale Tarn path with a suspected heart attack. Though the site was some way from the roadside, it was close enough to offer some hope that we could arrive in time to offer practical assistance. A Land Rover arrived from Ambleside base in spectacular time, and a couple more of us arrived together. We ran the 500 yards to the casualty site to find exactly the scenario which had been reported. The man had stopped breathing and had no pulse. Almost instinctively, we prepared the defib, cleared the man's shirt out of the way and I applied the pads. Dave Owen operated the machine and checked the readout, which confirmed that there was no heartbeat at all. We applied a shock, then another, and then another, stronger one. Each time, the man's body jerked abruptly, each time offering hope from an otherwise lifeless corpse. The ECG readout remained unmoved. He was quite dead, and nothing we could do would change that.

After the event, I thought about our actions and their consequences. We had undoubtedly attempted to revive the man with the best possible motives, but I thought of the man's wife, standing watching us. She must have felt a surge of hope as the sudden influx of rescuers and equipment arrived on scene. All those well-meaning, professional-looking (and acting) people, the shocks applied to her husband, the way he momentarily moved to the application of the electricity, the expectancy. And at the end of it all, nothing. I wonder whether it was right to subject her to that, no matter how well meaning our intentions. Where does hope end

197

and cold reality start in a situation like this? How long does a heart have to stop beating for us to let its owner lie in peace? Had his time come, as simple as that? Experienced medical staff might have the knowledge and experience to make informed judgements as to the worth of attempted revival using a defibrillator. I felt that we didn't have the ability to make that judgement and may have offered unjustified hope and intruded insensitively at a very private time.

One piece of equipment which has proved a raging success since its invention is the hot air breathing machine. In cases of hypothermia, the temperature of the body decreases steadily until loss of consciousness and eventually death occurs. Out on the hill, if a member of a group is suspected of being in the first stages of hypothermia, the golden rule is to stop immediately. Continuing the walk will further drain the energy resources of the casualty and lead to further loss of body heat and a worsening of the condition. Once stopped, the casualty has to be kept as warm as possible. An emergency shelter, bivvy bag or tent should be used to provide shelter and, contrary to older advice, wet clothing should be removed and replaced with dry. As much insulation from the ground as possible should be provided and other members of the group should snuggle up to the casualty to give extra warmth. (There may be a queue to perform this task depending on the sex of those involved!) A hot drink and high-energy, easily managed food should be given and assistance should be requested, even when the condition does not seem that serious, as deterioration can be quick and dangerous. In no circumstances should the casualty be warmed by rubbing or by giving alcohol. The result will be that heat is removed from the body's inner core and distributed to the extremities, from where it will be quickly lost, worsening the condition rapidly. It is at this point that the hot air breathing machine comes into its own. If we cannot warm the body well enough from the outside, we can warm it from the inside by providing a supply of hot air from a simple machine which is inhaled by the casualty.

The local press has mentioned at least two local inventors of this device, and I am sure there are more. The first reference to it came in 1975, when Peter Bell, he of Bell stretcher fame, invented a hot air breathing machine following an idea from Dr Evan Lloyd. The concept is simple. Carbon-dioxide is allowed to pass over crystals of soda lime, the resulting chemical reaction creating hot air, though not in the same quantities as is produced by team members on most call-outs. It's an extremely simple idea, and one which has helped many sufferers of hypothermia during the years. In milder cases, casualties have been observed to make fast and full recoveries in a very short time, whilst even those in a serious condition have improved so much it has amazed onlookers. Surprising then that the local newspaper ran another feature in 1983, attributing the invention of the hot air breathing machine to Mike Mitchell, a plumber who used parts of a home brew kit, plastic piping and a few bits and bobs from his business to produce effectively the same device as Peter Bell. The idea was passed to Mike by one of Edinburgh's leading anaesthetists, Dr Evan Lloyd. Sounds familiar. It attracted publicity after the device brought a sixteen-year-old fell walker back from close to death as his heart and lungs were failing due to extreme hypothermia. I have also heard claims from Wales for a similar device. All I can say is well done to all of them!

Stretcher-carrying was once the subject of much attention and design work. Bicycle wheels were mounted beneath the stretcher's frame to provide an easy carry with the option of wheeling the casualty over suitable terrain. Unfortunately, most mountain terrain proves too rough and rocky and, though great for those wild-eyed mountain-bikers who relish bone-jarring descents, most casualties would not thank us for the same experience. Other popularly used stretchers have had smooth wooden runners fitted beneath which allowed a convenient slide on snow, smooth grass or even on scree slopes. Again, one's casualty would need to be either minimally injured or a long way away with the fairies to cope with such rough handling.

The innovative warden of the Ullswater Outward Bound Centre,

Squadron Leader Lester Davies, developed an amazing motorised device which was capable of 'going up 1 in 3 gradients with the heaviest patients'. Sounds wonderful at first, but one has to bear in mind that the vast majority of rescues involve carrying the unfortunate casualties downhill, and that ascending 1 in 3 gradients is the last thing most rescue parties would want to do, in particular with 'the heaviest patients'! The Squadron Leader said at the time that, 'It takes hours to get them down the mountain to an ambulance. We depend on relays of stretcher-bearers, and frequently the patient is bumped and knocked around as we struggle to get the stretcher down.' His solution was the unconventional Ullswater Fellbounder. It was powered by a two-stroke engine and, bearing in mind its inventor's background, its single wheel was very appropriately derived from a Lancaster bomber! One hospital surgeon said at the time that 'anything that gets a person to hospital quickly is to be welcomed. This sounds a fine idea.' Well, it just shows how wrong you can be and, sadly, the Ullswater Fellbounder was eventually replaced by efficient rescuers and Sea King helicopters which, I ought to add, are without doubt capable of carrying the heaviest patients up 1 in 3 gradients!

One of the more recent developments for treating those with back or multiple injuries is the vacuum splint. It starts its journey to the casualty site as a floppy nylon bag filled with polystyrene balls, but is transformed into a rigid structure as air is pumped out of the sealed inner unit, creating a vacuum. In use, the bag is placed in its flaccid state next to the casualty, who is gently lifted onto it. The clever bit is that as the pump removes air and creates a rigid structure, the polystyrene balls shape themselves to the contours of the casualty, creating a splint which has effectively moulded itself to that person. This is considerably better than the old-fashioned back splint, which cannot adjust to this extent. Once the splint has settled and hardened, straps hold the casualty secure for placing on a stretcher for evacuation. This appears to be a great piece of kit, as long as it doesn't puncture!

Rescue teams also have a range of drugs available for removing pain. Probably the most commonly used is the gas nitrous oxide, or Entonox. Carried in a small cylinder fitted with a short pipe and breathing mask, the gas can be used in virtually all situations and has a rapid effect on the casualty, promoting a general feeling of well-being as well as reducing pain. Spare cylinders have to be carried in case the casualty requires the Entonox over a prolonged period, in which case they can get as high as kites but, despite periodic rumours, it is not true that rescue teams hold the occasional Entonox party! Other more serious drugs are also available, such as opiates which can be introduced via an injection into a suitable large muscle group such as the buttock or thigh, or more rapidly by a trained person via a line inserted into a vein. Other drugs are also carried, from the humble aspirin used for heart conditions, to Adrenalin and even antidotes to reverse any adverse reactions to drugs such as morphine.

These painkilling drugs can change the mood of a situation dramatically. I can recall one incident on Pavey Ark, in which a female climber had been pinned by a large boulder which had slipped down the gully beneath the foreboding East Wall. Her injuries included a badly broken leg and she was in a huge amount of pain, periodically screaming in agony and moaning. Whilst a few of us set up some anchor points ready for lowering the stretcher, others gave her medical attention, including an injection of Cyclomorph. To our relief, the screams ebbed until she fell silent for a while, only to surprise us somewhat when she started giggling and making the most outrageous comments. What a transformation!

Other specialist gear used by rescue teams includes splints which extend to apply traction, oxygen and resuscitation equipment, Propac monitors for constant evaluation of all the vital signs and a saw. But don't worry, that's only for removing the occasional obstructive branch. Which was exactly what was happening when the Langdale team suffered its most damaging incident involving an accident to its own members.

Stock Ghyll is a well-known beck and ravine above Ambleside, which even has its own 'To the Waterfalls' sign. For visitors and locals alike it provides a most pleasant woodland walk, and for more adventurous folk it is an exciting gorge scramble. The team had agreed to remove some branches which overhung the main gorge and which were inaccessible without the security offered by ropes and harnesses. A team training session had been arranged at the site, where other issues such as the methods of evacuation we would employ in the event of an accident here could be discussed. Some team members would abseil down and remove the offending branches at the same time.

The bleepers went off midway through the evening, with an urgent-sounding voice requesting assistance in Stock Ghyll. The levels of seriousness of any situation can often be clearly heard through someone's voice and this sounded serious. I picked Martin up on the way past his house, and neither of us had any doubt that the incident involved the team. There was almost a sense of desperation at the accident site, far removed from the calm and detached manner in which most call-outs are dealt with. Some individuals in the team were almost panicked, and needed to be calmed down. An over emotional approach can lead to mistakes and irrationality.

Two rescuers were injured, Brendan and Phil, both as a result of a rockfall which had occurred in the area where the branches were being removed. A steep bank led down to the edge of the beck, where a short vertical step barred easy access and egress. Whilst those team members present in the gorge bottom stabilised things as best they could, we fixed ropes to allow others to descend safely with more equipment and to prepare for the evacuation. Things settled down a bit and, ably assisted by Colyn Earnshaw and Martin, we soon had the gorge side roped and ready for hoisting the two casualties out. We used manpower rather than any complicated hoisting methods to raise the stretchers from the gully bed, and each was gently lifted clear and into the willing arms of other rescuers who carried them out of the woods to the waiting ambulances.

202

It was a fairly straightforward rescue, but it had a profound effect on the team. There was a reluctance to carry out an effective post-mortem on the exercise, despite it being obvious that there were some lessons to be learnt, and the incident was hushed up as much as possible. Looking at things logically and impartially, the accident should never have been allowed to happen. The injured men were hit by a rockfall from about thirty feet up, a rockfall which would have been difficult but not impossible to foresee, if a reasonable examination of the rock face had been carried out initially. But, one has to question the general safety standards employed when rescuers were allowed to stand beneath a cliff face upon which work was being carried out. Most climbers will tell you where the most dangerous part of a climb is – at the bottom where you are a target for any stone which may be dislodged or equipment which may be dropped. It was a hard way for a simple lesson to be learnt.

The only light moment during the entire proceedings came after the rescue had taken place, when we had to arrange to inform the wives of those involved. Graham Hartley, our sensitive and personable vicar was suggested as the conveyor of tidings. But fortunately someone had the presence of mind to quash this idea very quickly. The arrival of the vicar on the scene could only suggest one thing to the recipients of his visit! As Brendan and Phil were well in the land of the living, the duty was performed by others whose presence would bode less ill.

With rescuers being trained to an ever increasing level, it is interesting to speculate on the future of mountain rescue in general. After all, there is a limit to how much a volunteer can be trained, both in terms of the time available and in terms of the individual's aptitude and ability. Many people are not aware that mountain rescue work is purely voluntary, and the teams retain a great deal of autonomy in an age when accountability is the buzzword. The Langdale/Ambleside team has over forty volunteer members from a wide variety of backgrounds. A quick glance down the list reveals council employees (the Langdale team has one who regularly turns up for rescues in his overalls and steel toecapped boots and still beats most people to the accident site), a playground engineer, shopkeepers, doctors, outdoor pursuits instructors, a carpenter and a butcher, National Trust wardens and National Park rangers, teachers, engineers, sales ladies and a film cameraman. Some of these people have little in common outside their rescue work and a love of the hills, and relationships within rescue teams can be as strained as in any workplace. But they bring a wide range of skills into the team. Some are expert climbers, others just strong fell walkers. Some are engineers or electricians and can maintain complex equipment which would otherwise cost a fortune to maintain. Others put their efforts into promoting mountain safety, raising money or simply sitting on the committee, sharing the decisions which are made.

What is clear is that it is completely unrealistic to expect all these people to train as paramedics or expert climbers. Some will have the ability, many will not. So if rescue teams retain their current voluntary status, how can they improve? Busy rescue teams already demand so much time from their members, is it realistic to expect them to give more? Equally, are members of the public receiving the best service they could get? The answer to the last question is a guarded yes – in the current circumstances they are, but there is no doubt that the service could be improved.

It can up its standards in a small way by improving training methods and using funds to employ more professional trainers. Communication methods can be fine-tuned, local knowledge worked upon, and many other details tightened up, but the service can only be improved significantly by the introduction of full time paid rescuers, backed up with the services of a helicopter.

I base this premise on the following facts. Firstly, the speed at which the casualty site is reached by the busier teams is quite remarkable for a voluntary group, and can realistically only be bettered by the deployment of helicopter assistance. In some circumstances, this could be a life-saving measure. Secondly, the only way massively to improve the medical skills of rescuers is for them to undergo full time medical training, similar to that undertaken by paramedics. This cannot be done on a part time volunteer basis, and would have to become the responsibility of a full time rescue service. Likewise, technical mountaineering skills beyond the ability to be a reliable and strong fell walker have to be worked for and, at present, only a small number of rescuers who are either climbing instructors or high standard climbers through their personal interest are able to fulfil this requirement. A full time rescue service would be professional in every sense of the word, and would eliminate the high numbers of relatively incompetent personnel to be found in most teams. This statement should not be taken out of context as each and every member of every rescue team currently has an important part to play, but at the sharp end of the rescue service there is no room for incompetence.

If such a service were to be set up in an area such as the Lake District, two fundamental problems would have to be tackled. The first concerns finance. Both rescuers and the general public do not want the imposition of insurance schemes, but the money would have to come from somewhere in the form of grants, sponsorship, public subscription or whatever. The second problem is that if a centrally positioned full time rescue team were set up for example, at Ambleside, there would be many occasions on which additional assistance would be required. Helicopters get grounded in bad weather, searches and long carries require large numbers of personnel, so therefore a back-up service would be required. I wonder how viable this would be when a centrally positioned elite unit is tackling most of the work, only calling on the rest to assist when conditions are particularly bad or when a certain type of incident occurs. Much goodwill would probably disappear and infrequent rescue work would tend to fragment and disenchant.

Bearing this in mind, perhaps the current system is not too bad and it has at least one aspect which places it beyond any normal emergency service or sport and on a parallel with the lifeboat service, which is that assistance to those in distress is provided by others who pursue the same risks – sailor helps sailor and mountaineer helps mountaineer. In a modern society whose values seem to have gone sadly astray, this is a reassuring symbol of humanity and goodwill, and all the volunteers who put in so much time and effort on behalf of the mountain rescue services deserve recognition for this as well as for the quality of the service they provide.

GLOSSARY

Abseil: a method of controlled sliding down the rope to enable a descent to be made over steep ground.

Arête: a sharp ridge, or rib of rock.

To belay: to safeguard other climbers in a roped group by tying oneself to a firm anchor point.

Belay platform: otherwise known as a stance, a ledge on which the climber anchors himself in order to safeguard the other climbers.

Belay point: an anchor, usually placed by the climber but sometimes *in situ*, to which the climber can tie for security.

Belay, running: *see* **Running belay**

To bivvy: to sleep out on a mountainside without the benefit of full camping gear.

Bivvy bag: a cover to enhance your prospects of surviving a bivvy comfortably. In its most basic form, a large plastic bag, and at the other end of the spectrum, a specially designed Gore-tex shelter.

Bolts: usually expansion bolts drilled into the rock face to which a karabiner can be attached for protection.

Chimney: a cleft in the rock face usually between approximately one and six feet wide.

Chimneying: a technique used for ascending chimneys, involving jamming knees, back, feet and arms to aid upward progress.

Cornice: overhanging mass of snow at the top of the leeward side of a slope, created by wind.

Crack system: a series of splits or cracks in the rock which can be linked together to form the basis of a climb.

Crampons: metal spikes which fasten to the sole of the boot to enable easy progress on hard snow or ice.

A Desmond Decker: slang for a fall to the ground.

Entonox: nitrous oxide, or laughing gas, used as a pain killer.

Friends: very clever devices which consist of four semi-circular cams which can contract or expand. The climber places the Friend into a crack and allows the cams to expand against the crack sides. The harder the stem which links the cams is pulled outwards, the greater the force pushing the cams outwards. Friends have enabled parallel-sided cracks to be climbed safely and have revolutionised climbing safety.

GBS (Global Positioning System): new electronic equipment which uses satellites to fix positions. The device will accurately pinpoint your location anywhere in the world by locking onto three different satellites and giving a readout. Though highly accurate, they do not replace traditional map and compass skills for mountaineers.

Grades: climbs are given grades to indicate the level of difficulty. The easiest climbing grade is Moderate, the next Difficult (Diff), followed by Very Difficult (V Diff), Severe, Very Severe (VS), Hard Very Severe (Hard VS), and Extremely Severe. The final grade is subdivided into 'E' grades of increasing difficulty, E1, E2, etc. to E9 at present. Abbreviations in brackets are those normally used by the climbing fraternity.

Gully: a bigger version of a chimney, often several hundred feet high.

Harness: a device which fastens around the climber's waist and legs and to which the rope is attached. It spreads the forces created in a fall onto different parts of the body, and is very comfortable to sit in whilst suspended from a rope, when abseiling for example.

Hypothermia: a condition which occurs when the body cannot produce sufficient heat to replace that which is lost (to cold, wet, windy conditions). High levels of energy use through physical exertion is often a contributory factor in mountain situations. If left untreated death can occur.

Jumar clamps: devices which clip to the rope and which can slide upwards, but not down. Their primary use is for ascending ropes.

Karrimat: closed cell foam which acts as a barrier to water and cold. Usually used for sleeping on (or sitting on for lunch).

Karabiner: a metal linking device which is extensively used in climbing. Usually oval or D-shaped, they have a gate on one side which opens to allow ropes, slings, etc. to be clipped in. A vital part of the climbing safety chain.

Layback holds: holds which are used to pull sideways on, rather than downwards. The feet usually have to push in opposition for progress upwards to be made.

Mantelshelf: a mantelshelf, or mantelshelf move, is one made when a climber is trying to gain a high ledge. It involves pulling up, then transferring the force in the hands to a pushing position until one foot can be placed on the ledge and the rest of the body balances up after.

Névé: hard snow which has an icy consistency, normally the result of extensive freeze/thaw action. Great for climbing on.

Pacman sac: a rucsac containing medical equipment and basic survival gear used to take to the casualty by those first present on a rescue call-out.

Pegs: metal pins which are hammered into the rock to provide anchor points. Also known as **Pitons**.

Nuts: metal wedges of many sizes and shapes which are hand-placed into cracks in the rock to provide anchors and running belays.

Protection: term used by climbers to generally describe the equipment used to provide running belays.

Prussik knot: a knot used for ascending ropes. Correctly tied, the knot will slide up the rope, but will not slide down once tensioned.

Rope-length: most climbing ropes are 165 feet long, so if you run out a rope-length, you will have climbed about 165 feet.

Running belay: an anchor point placed by the lead climber through which his or her rope runs. Each running belay, or runner as they are known, can prevent a fall to the ground. If a climber falls off while five feet above a runner, he or she will fall a total of ten feet, plus rope stretch.

Slings: very strong bands of nylon tape which are stitched together to form loops. Used for placing over spikes of rock, around trees, etc. to provide anchor points.

Stance: *see* **Belay platform**

Thrutching: a climbing term which describes the motions required to climb tight chimneys, when the body must be moved upwards a bit at a time in a constricted environment.

Traverse: a horizontal movement on a climb.

Undercut crack: a horizontal fissure into which the climber can place his hands and pull outwards.

White out: conditions in which heavy snow and mist conspire to produce a whiteness in which any sort of meaningful vision is impossible to obtain. Visibility may be just one or two metres and it will be virtually impossible to distinguish up from down.

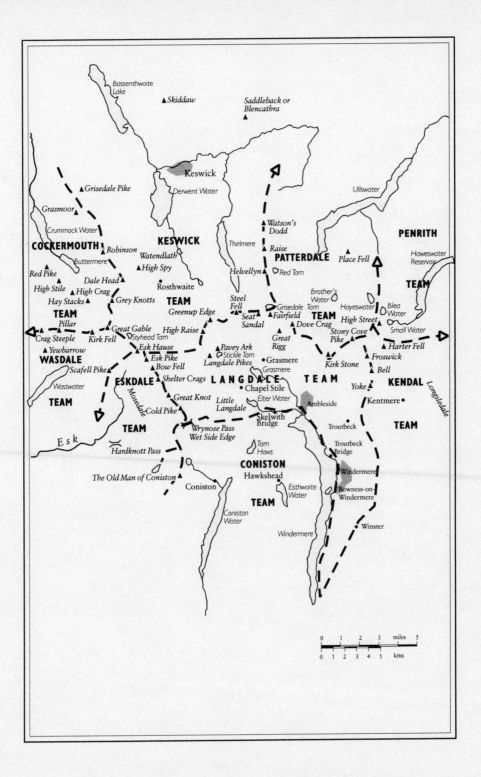